GREEK
DECLAMATION

GREEK DECLAMATION

D. A. RUSSELL

READER IN CLASSICAL LITERATURE AND
FELLOW OF ST JOHN'S COLLEGE,
OXFORD

CAMBRIDGE UNIVERSITY PRESS
CAMBRIDGE
LONDON   NEW YORK   NEW ROCHELLE
MELBOURNE   SYDNEY

Published by the Press Syndicate of the University of Cambridge
The Pitt Building, Trumpington Street, Cambridge CB2 1RP
32 East 57th Street, New York, NY 10022, USA
296 Beaconsfield Parade, Middle Park, Melbourne 3206, Australia

© Cambridge University Press 1983

First published 1983

Printed in Great Britain by the University Press, Cambridge

Library of Congress catalogue card number: 83–7270

British Library Cataloguing in Publication Data
Russell, D. A.
Greek declamation.
1. Greek orations–History and criticism
I. Title
888'. 0108   PA3263
ISBN 0 521 25780 8

Contents

	Preface	vii
1	Evidence, definitions, origins	1
2	Sophistopolis, or the world of the Aristeus	21
3	Teachers and theories	40
4	Performers and occasions	74
5	Character and characters	87
6	Declamation and history	106
	Bibliography	129
	Indexes	133

Preface

The impulse to write on this subject came from the invitation to deliver the Gray Lectures at Cambridge in 1981. So my thanks are first due to the Faculty Board of Classics, its officers, and the audience of the lectures, all of whom contributed to my pleasure in the experience. I have not sought to remove the tone of a lecture altogether; but I have added much, particularly the account of the relevant parts of *stasis*-theory in chapter 3, which is essential for understanding what the declaimers were about, but not promising material for a series of afternoon *epideixeis*.

My other great obligation is to my Oxford colleagues, Michael Winterbottom and Doreen Innes. They have generously allowed me to use their work on the text of Sopatros' *Diaireseis Zetematon*, including their collation of C (= Corpus Christi College Oxford 90), an important MS, dated by N. G. Wilson to about 1330, and not used by previous editors. Their materials for a new text will be published in a forthcoming supplement of the *Bulletin of the Institute of Classical Studies*. I am further in their debt for much help in revising and enriching what I have written; but for all errors and inadequacies I am of course solely responsible.

Some aspects of this subject figure in G. A. Kennedy's *Greek Rhetoric under Christian Emperors* (1983), especially pp. 73–86 and 133–179. This book appeared too late for me to do more than recommend it in general and add a few references to it in footnotes.

Oxford 1983   D. A. R.

I
Evidence, definitions, origins

> Graecus rhetor, quod genus stultorum amabilissimum est.
> 'A Greek rhetor, the nicest kind of fool.'
>
> Seneca

I

Pretending to be someone else, and composing imaginary speeches in character, is an essential part of most literary activity. It is important not only in drama, epic and fiction, but also, at least in ancient times, in lyric poetry, history and philosophy. But it also has an educational function. Where public speech is important (as in the Greco-Roman world), it is important to train people in its skills. What better way than by inventing situations and giving one's pupils parts to play? And, since what is taught in school has at least some impact on what people do elsewhere, the practice, like other rhetorical practices, may be expected to have an influence on literature; and it is for this reason that scholars other than specialist students of rhetoric have found it of interest.

In Latin literature, therefore, this sort of exercise, under the name of *declamatio*, has been much studied; indeed, it has a recognized place in the histories of literature.[1] It is received wisdom that, somewhere in the second half of the first century B.C., it suddenly became very popular and influential. The main evidence for this is the work of the elder Seneca,[2] a collection of excerpts from the *Controversiae* (imaginary court cases) and

---

[1] Bonner (1949) ch. 8; D. W. T. C. Vessey in *Cambridge History of Classical Literature* (1982) II.499; Winterbottom (1980) 59–61.

[2] The most convenient and informative edition is Winterbottom (1974). The two most recent monographs (Sussman 1978, Fairweather 1981) complement each other.

Suasoriae (imaginary deliberative speeches) which he had heard from the famous declaimers of his youth and finally wrote down for his sons in his old age. Seneca is a beguiling author. His gossipy charms give a seductive introduction to this corner of the literary world. Here are portrayed many enthusiasts, some eccentrics, and some who were figures of significance in the literary life of the time: notably, of course, the young Ovid, in whose poetry rhetorical techniques are peculiarly obvious and all-pervading.[3]

It is, I think, Seneca, particularly in the more 'literary' parts of his work, who is mainly responsible for the view that 'declamation' had a powerful influence on poetic practice and on other forms of literature. There is no doubt that this is true enough of certain poets, Ovid and Juvenal in particular, but also Lucan. These all display evident signs of declamatory experience, and frequently write with precisely the type of sharp wit that one associates with declamation. But the way in which this influence is usually described is misleading. Critics talk of figures, *loci communes*, methods of transition and features of style; thus J. de Decker's famous *Iuvenalis Declamans*[4] sees the contribution of the declaimers to Juvenal as lying in these, and in the example they set of a loose form of composition, admitting every kind of rhetorically attractive purple patch. Now Seneca does give this impression. His concentration is on detail rather than organization, on *sententiae* and *colores* rather than on planning and argument. But the essence of the exercise is not here at all. What is really specific to declamation, rather than to other forms of rhetorical exercise, is its firm organization. What the young men learned at this stage in their education was how to shape the effective elements of a case into a planned whole, in which descriptions and *loci communes* did indeed have a place, but a determinate one which they were not supposed to exceed.[5] So Seneca has, I think,

---

[3] For Ovid, see esp. *Contr.* 2.2.8–12. Ovid was friendly with Seneca's close friend Junius Gallio (*Suas.* 3.7). That he was heavily influenced by rhetorical teaching is obvious and well known (e.g. Bonner [1949] 149). In reverse, Seneca's interest in poetry should be noted: see esp. *Suas.* 1.19, 6.24, where he cites poetical passages as examples of the treatment of a set theme.

[4] *Iuvenalis Declamans* dates from 1913, but lies behind much more recent work.

[5] Cf ps.-Dionysius, *Ars rhetorica* 10 (372 U–R): ἐνίοις κἀκεῖνο ἁμάρτημα, αἱ καλούμεναι ἐκφράσεις, πολλαχοῦ τὸ χειμῶνα γράφειν καὶ λοιμοὺς καὶ λιμοὺς καὶ

Evidence, definitions, origins

fathered an error: the rhetorical features we find in the poets are not, as a rule, due specifically to declamatory experience, but to rhetorical training in general. Whether Seneca knew better may be debated. A certain mystery surrounds his apparent ignorance of the main stream of Greek rhetorical teaching. But it is of course perfectly possible that he took the general principles of the exercise for granted, and omits the fundamental theory of 'types of issue' (*staseis*) not out of ignorance, but because he chose to concentrate rather on the sort of detail which he felt would be attractive and memorable.

These doubts concerning Seneca encourage investigation of the Greek tradition itself. Everything about the exercises makes it clear that they were a Greek invention, dating back well before Seneca's time. They continued well into the Byzantine era. Most of our Greek evidence is indeed much later than Seneca; but the coincidences between it and the Roman evidence can only be due to a common source. Greeks did not learn from Romans — least of all in rhetoric.

2

The surviving Greek evidence is in fact very extensive, and ranges over many centuries. It is, however, a small fraction of what once existed. On certain centres and periods, we are fairly well-informed (Athens and the Ionian cities in the second century of our era, Antioch in the fourth, Gaza in the sixth) but it was not only in the places we know, but throughout the Greco-Roman world that this art of declamation flourished, both dominating education (moral as well as rhetorical) and playing a large part in the development of literature. We have, on the one hand, finished speeches, meant to endure; on the other, instructions and summaries by teachers in the schools.

(i) To the former category belong a certain number of papyri,

παρατάξεις καὶ ἀριστείας... τοῦτο δὲ τὸ πάθημα ἀνθρώπων ἀγνοούντων ὅτι καὶ ἐν τοῖς ἐπικαίροις τῶν ἀγώνων ἔστι φαντασίας κίνησις ἱκανὴ καὶ οὐ δεῖ ἔξωθεν λόγοις φαντασίας ἐπεισκυκλεῖσθαι. ('Some suffer also from the fault of what are called 'descriptions', i.e. frequent depiction of storm, pestilences, famines, battles and heroic actions... This is the error of people who do not see that there is sufficient excitement of the imagination in the essential points of the dispute, and there is no need for imaginative visualizations to be wheeled in to the speech from outside.')

some Hellenistic in date, which testify to the composition of *suasoriae* and historical *controversiae* from quite an early period: *P. Hibeh* 15 (third century B.C.) advocates action against Alexander,[6] *P. Berol.* 9781 (same period) contains a speech meant to form part of the Leptines case known from Demosthenes.[7] But then there comes a long gap. Our next group of actual texts is from the Second Sophistic. There are three *suasoriae* — one with a definite historical setting, two vague exhortations to battle — attributed to Lesbonax of Mytilene;[8] there are the declamations of the famous sophist Polemon of Laodicea in which the fathers of two heroes of Marathon dispute the honour of delivering the funeral oration over the fallen; and there is at any rate one piece, of a fairly sensational kind, by Adrian of Tyre.[9] There are also some light pieces by Lucian, notably the speeches for and against the acceptance of Phalaris' bull at Delphi; and the entertaining 'Court of the Vowels' in which Sigma charges Tau with robbing him of all words spelt with double *tau*.[10] Here grammar and rhetoric join forces for the schoolboy's delectation. But these are small things compared with the elaborate historical declamations of Aristides. Some call these 'Lesereden', as though they were to be read and not delivered; and indeed the density of the thought suggests this.[11] The most famous set is the 'Leuctrian'

[6] *P. Hibeh* 15 is published also in Jacoby, *FGrHist* 105A6, though it is clearly a rhetorical exercise and not part of a history. There are many later papyri of declamations: see Jander (1913), R. A. Pack, *The Greek and Latin Literary Texts from Graeco-Roman Egypt*, ed. 2 (1965), nos. 2495–2559, and esp. *P. Yale* 1729 (= *Yale Papyri* II no. 105, ed. S. H. Stephens), an important historical declamation dated to the first century A.D.

[7] See below, ch. 6, n. 5.

[8] Ed. F. Kiehr (1907); see Reardon (1971) 106. Philostratus' account of Polemon is in *Lives of the Sophists* (= *VS*) 530ff (= 106ff Wright).

[9] Adrian: Philostratus, *VS* 585ff (= 222ff Wright). Text of declamations in Hinck's Polemon, also in *RG* I.526ff. The only genuine piece is fr. 1, about a suspected woman poisoner and another woman who promises to burn her and is therefore herself suspected of poisoning. Other pieces assigned to Adrian come from Iamblichus' *Babyloniaca*, a romance (ed. E. Habrich [1960] fr. 1.35.101).

[10] On Lucian's *Phalaris* see B. Keil, *Hermes* XLVIII (1913) 494ff; J. Bompaire (1958) 265ff.

[11] On Aristides' speeches as *Lesereden*, see W. Morel, *RE* XV.1.497. Aristides himself (*Or.* 50.26) reports a divine command given him 'to weave speech with bare thought as with words', and uses the term πολύνοια of this. It is natural

Evidence, definitions, origins 5

speeches, in which advocates of support for Thebes oppose supporters of Sparta and of neutrality in the Athens of 370 B.C. Notable also are the 'Sicilian' speeches, based on the events of 415–413, and the 'Embassy to Achilles', in which the speaker seeks to turn Achilles' anger against the Trojans and not against his own people.[12] Aristides became a classic, and later rhetors often answered and developed his themes. Among them was Libanius of Antioch, the greatest orator and teacher of the fourth century, in whose extant works are no less than fifty-one declamations, only a handful of them not genuine.[13] Some of these are historical (the 'Apology of Socrates' is the most elaborate[14]), some serious *plasmata* – fictitious cases – and some frankly comic; these last, in which morose old men and misers parade their bizarre characteristics in absurd situations, are the most attractive of the collection, and have had a certain influence on modern literature; Ben Jonson's Morose in *The Silent Woman* seems to come from *Declamation 26*. Whether it is because of this frivolity, or because of some more arcane lack of technique, Libanius had a poor reputation with some of his successors: Eunapius thought him 'feeble' and ignorant of what every schoolboy knows.[15] His contemporary Himerius, less urbane and Attic in style, but more forceful and grandiose, is known to us largely from the excerpts in Photius, though a few extracts have survived independently.[16] He taught at Athens, and had influential pupils; moreover, he lays claim to some family connection with Plutarch, almost three centuries before him. Finally, a pleasing surprise. Choricius of Gaza, who lived in the

---

to connect this with his deliberately packed thought, reminiscent often of Thucydides' speeches.

[12] Boulanger (1923) ch. 5, esp. 157ff; G. A. Kennedy in Bowersock (1974) 20ff; Reardon (1971) 99ff. The Sicilian speeches have been well edited by Pernot (1981); for the 'Embassy of Achilles' see Kindstrand (1973) 215ff. Aristides was much studied by the later declaimers: see (e.g.) *RG* VIII.188, 346 (Sopatros).

[13] The *Declamations* are in vols. V–VII of Foerster's Libanius. See now Kennedy (1983) 150ff. [14] See Markowski (1910).

[15] Eunapius, *Lives of the Philosophers*, 496.

[16] Wernsdorf's commentary (1790) still usefully supplements the modern edition by A. Colonna (1951). Kennedy (1983) 141ff concentrates on the epideictic speeches.

sixth century, may well be judged the best of these writers.[17] He is a great stylistic virtuoso, able to write elegant and classical Attic with full observance of the accentual clausulae of his own day. Furthermore, he delights and instructs not only by his actual speeches but by the elegant prefaces in which he lays bare the secrets of his art.[18]

(ii) Choricius' work is both educational and literary, evidence perhaps of how hard it is to separate the two. Much of our knowledge of school practice, however, comes from technical treatises which do no more than allude to or briefly narrate the problems which the pupil is set. Most of these treatises are concerned with *staseis*, that is to say 'types of issue'. Once again, the Hellenistic material is mostly lost: Hermagoras of Temnos, the most important early authority, is known only from allusions in later texts.[19] *Ad Herennium* and Cicero's *De inventione*, however, tell us a good deal: both are purely Greek in inspiration, except that they often take their examples from Roman affairs. Our main Greek source is much later. It is Hermogenes of Tarsus, a youthful prodigy of the time of Marcus Aurelius, worn out by the age of twenty-five.[20] So far as we can see, he made few substantial innovations, but codified and illustrated the theory in a form that became classic; his predecessors, and his contemporary rival Minucianus,[21] fade from the scene; his later commentators,

---

[17] Gaza had become a Christian city under Bishop Porphyrius (396–420), whose *Life* (by Mark the Deacon) is among the most revealing documents of the age. In the fifth and sixth centuries it developed a flourishing literary and philosophical life; besides Choricius, Procopius, Johannes and Aeneas were notable; see now Kennedy (1983) 169ff.

[18] For later declamation, see Hunger (1978) 1.93ff. The many references to declamation in the later commentaries on Hermogenes testify to a familiarity with the idea of this sort of exercise, but not necessarily to much practice of it.

[19] Hermagoras: D. Matthes, *Lustrum* III (1958) 58–214, 262–78.

[20] See, besides Jäneke (1904), Kennedy, *ARRW* 619–33. On Hermogenes' stylistic doctrine (*Peri Ideōn*), see Hagedorn (1964). Life in Philostratus, *VS* 577 (= 204 Wright): he was said to be ἐν παισὶ μὲν γέρων, ἐν δὲ γηράσκουσι παῖς ('an old man among children, a child among the ageing').

[21] Minucianus of Athens, distantly related to Plutarch, flourished *c.* 150; a younger Minucianus, of the same family, was active as a teacher in the third century, and is probably the author of the extant treatise on *epicheirēmata* (340ff Sp.–H.).

Evidence, definitions, origins 7

who treat his words as they would a classical text, include the philosopher Syrianus[22] and the rhetor Sopatros, under whose name is preserved a vast collection of 'questions' which is the most important source of all. This Sopatros, who taught at Athens, had a son (or pupil?) called Carponianus, and alleges some connection with Himerius.[23] His collection comprises over eighty themes, arranged according to *stasis* and (for the most part) worked out in great detail. The arrangement is mainly Hermogenes', but in some respects he apparently follows Minucianus.[24] We supplement this tradition, in which *stasis*-theory is always the guiding principle, from one or two rhetors who have other concerns: Apsines[25] and ps.-Dionysius[26] are the chief of these.

[22] Syrianus, the teacher of Proclus, wrote commentaries on large parts of Aristotle's *Metaphysics*, as well as on Hermogenes. Proclus' debt to Syrianus is discussed with particular reference to the theory of poetry by Sheppard (1980).

[23] The clues to Sopatros' life and career are slight. Carponianus (*RG* VIII.78) is apparently a military man in imperial service (not in *PLRE*); unless the address υἱέ indicates an intellectual or spiritual 'son' or pupil (a Christian usage, with a clearly religious flavour, to which I know no Greek parallel from rhetoric or other secular arts, though for Latin *mi fili* cf Gellius 13.20.5, Apuleius, *Apology* 72.3, 97.1), he really was the author's son. Rhetors naturally often bred rhetors (cf n. 21, n. 25, and Himerius with his son Rufinus). The connection with ὁ σοφὸς ὁ ἡμέτερος Ἱμέριος ('our wise man, Himerius': so C at *RG* VIII.318.29 [see Preface]) means no more, in my judgement, than that Sopatros taught at Athens, not that he had any particularly close relationship with Himerius. It cannot therefore be used to prove a fourth-century date, and the great *Diaireseis Zētēmatōn* ('Divisions of Questions': this form and meaning of the title is to be preferred to that given by Russell and Wilson, *Menander Rhetor*, 226) may well be a good deal later. Boulanger (1923) 456 n. 3, confidently says 'fin du VIᵉ siècle', but this can hardly be right – it would put him later than Choricius. Whether the Sopatros of the *Diaireseis* is the same as the author of notes on Hermogenes given under this name in *RG* IV and V is an open question, with a good deal to be said against the identification. He is anyway distinct from the philosopher Sopatros of Apamea, a pupil of Iamblichus, who may be his grandfather.

[24] His order of the types of 'antithetical' cases (*antistasis, metastasis, antenklēma, syngnōmē*) is said to be Minucianus' (*RG* V.173). Note also the position of *pragmatika* following *metalēpsis* (*RG* VIII.286).

[25] Valerius Apsines of Gadara (third century A.D.) also taught at Athens and also had a son (Onasimos) to follow him in his profession. Text of his *technē*, 217ff Sp.–H.; cf Kennedy, *ARRW* 633ff.

[26] Text in Dionysius, *Opuscula* 2.253–387. Translation of chapters on epideictic in Russell and Wilson, *Menander Rhetor*, 362ff; other short extracts in Russell (1981) 183f, with discussion, ibid. 9ff. For the chapters dealing with declamation,

We thus know a good deal about the practice of declamation in the Greek schools of the late Empire. For the earlier period – the heyday of the Second Sophistic in the second century A.D. – we have, as well as the contemporary declamations of Aristides and others, the instructive and amusing anecdotal tradition preserved in Philostratus' *Lives of the Sophists*.[27] And we have also, of course, the Latin sources: not only can inferences about Greek practice be drawn from Seneca, Quintilian[28] and Calpurnius Flaccus,[29] but Seneca names and quotes some twenty-five Greek rhetors of Augustan or earlier date.[30] What he says is tantalizingly

see D. A. Russell in *Entretiens Hardt* XXV (1979) 113–34; see also below, ch. 3, p. 72. The sections on *logoi eschēmatismenoi* ('figured speeches') are also important; cf K. Schöpsdau, *Hermes* CXVIII (1975) 122f. See also below pp. 72f.

[27] Cf Bowersock (1969) 1–16, Reardon (1971) 115ff.

[28] A commentary on the *Minor Declamations* by M. Winterbottom is near publication; the *Major Declamations* have much less claim to come from Quintilian's school, but are fuller and more entertaining.

[29] Calpurnius Flaccus gives very brief statements of themes and salient points. A much later set of Latin declamations by Ennodius, bishop of Pavia in the early sixth century, seems to contain a good deal of Greek material, despite the general decline in knowledge of Greek in the West at that time.

[30] Bornecque (1902) lists all the declaimers in Seneca, including the Greek ones, and uses earlier work. It may suffice here to mention some who are especially notable (for refs. to Seneca, see the Index in Winterbottom's edition). (i) Adaios, 'rhetor ex Asianis non proiecti nominis', probably the same as an epigrammatist from Macedonia known from *Anth. Pal.* 7.51, 238, 240, 694; a quotation from his 'Tyrannicide released by pirates' (*Contr.* 1.7.18) shows poetical words (ταχινός, ἀντιάω). (ii) Aemilianus, perhaps the man mentioned by Plutarch, *De defectu* 17. (iii) Artemon, from whom Sen. quotes a blatantly 'Asianic' passage, *Suas.* 1.11, on Alexander: βουλευόμεθα εἰ χρὴ περαιοῦσθαι. οὐ ταῖς Ἑλλησποντίαις ἠόσιν ἐφεστῶτες οὐδ' ἐπὶ τῷ Παμφυλίῳ πελάγει τὴν ἐμπρόθεσμον καραδοκοῦμεν ἄμπωτιν· οὐδὲ Εὐφράτης τοῦτ' ἔστιν οὐδὲ Ἰνδός, ἀλλ' εἴτε γῆς τέρμα εἴτε φύσεως ὅρος εἴτε πρεσβύτατον στοιχεῖον εἴτε γένεσις θεῶν, ἱερώτερόν ἐστιν ἢ κατὰ ναῦς ὕδωρ. ('We are debating if we must cross. We are not standing on the shore of the Hellespont nor by the Pamphylian sea, awaiting the punctual tide; this is no Euphrates or Indus; be it earth's end or nature's bound, oldest element or gods' origin, it is a water too holy for ships.') (iv) Dorion, the author of a metaphrasis of parts of Homer (*Suas.* 1.12) as well as declamations: an extravagant writer, characteristically employed (*Contr.* 10.5.23) on the theme of 'Parrhasius using the prisoner of war as a model for Prometheus in torment': τίς Οἰδίπους ἔσται, τίς Ἀτρεύς; οὐ γράψεις γὰρ ἂν μὴ μύθους ἴδῃς ζῶντας ('Who will be your Oedipus or your Atreus? You won't paint them unless you have seen the myths in the flesh.') (v) Gorgias, the teacher of Cicero's son, and probably author of

Evidence, definitions, origins

brief, but enough to show two things: the rhetors of that time, especially those labelled *Asiani*, indulged rather more in daring conceits than their successors did, and also allowed themselves somewhat more moral licence in the choice and treatment of their themes. The gang-rape of the young male transvestite who is thereafter banned from speaking in public is the sort of thing which later taste seems to have rejected, though homosexual prostitution does play a part at all periods. To Seneca, the Greek rhetors were 'the most lovable kind of fools'; his general contempt for them keeps coming through.[31]

3

So far, I have been using the Latin-derived term 'declamation' and its subdivisions *controversia* and *suasoria*. *Declamatio*, as its name suggests, should originally denote an exercise in delivery rather than in composition. Perhaps, therefore, as a late Greek–Latin vocabulary suggests, the Romans used the word to represent the Greek *anaphōnēsis* (ἀναφώνησις).[32] If so, it means properly a voice exercise, such as orators and actors used to keep themselves in trim. But a natural semantic development led to its being used for the speech composed to be delivered in training, not for the delivery of it. The English word 'exercise' has a

---

the treatise on 'fingers' of which we have a partial Latin version by Rutilius Lupus (ed. E. Brooks, 1970). (vi) Hermagoras (not the earlier Hermagoras of Temnos, the main author of '*stasis*-theory'), a pupil of Theodorus: *Contr.* 10.1.15 attributes to him the notable phrase κτίσωμεν ἰδίᾳ, ὦ πένητες, πόλιν ('Poor Men, let us found a city on our own' (cf below ch. 2, §3)). (vii) Hybreas of Mylasa, a powerful man in Caria, whose rococo 'Asianic' style pleased Antony (Plutarch, *Ant.* 24) and who continued active in politics in the thirties. (viii) Lesbocles of Mitylene, less successful rival of his fellow-countryman Potamon, who served on embassies to Rome in Caesar's time and again in 25 B.C., and wrote encomia of Brutus and Caesar; between them, these sophists, with the poet Crinagoras, established Lesbos as an important literary centre (Bowersock [1965] 11, 36, 86). (ix) Nicetes, famous for his *impetus*. Little is known of these apart from what Seneca tells us; but widespread practice of declamation is certain.

[31] *Contr.* 5.6 (gang-rape); 10.5.25 (fools).
[32] *CGL* III 351.65 (Hermeneumata Stephani): declamatio ἀναφώνησις. Cf Bonner (1949) 20 and (1977) 73. For ἀναφώνησις as a voice exercise, see Galen, *De sanitate tuenda* 1, Plutarch, *Mor.* 1071C.

similar ambiguity; so has the nearest Greek equivalent, *meletē* (μελέτη).³³

But *meletē*, when it means an actual composition, is usually limited in its denotation both by content and by construction. Not everything delivered by way of exercise is a *meletē* in this strict sense. Two conditions must be fulfilled: it has to be the reproduction either of a forensic speech or of a deliberative one; and it has to be a complete oration, not just part of one.

The first limitation means that encomia and other 'epideictic' forms do not count. This is made clear by Menander³⁴ at the beginning of his treatise on epideictic speeches, where he excludes from his subject the display of practical oratory which the 'sophists' make, because they are 'not a demonstration (*epideixis*) but practice in cases (*meletē agōnōn*)'. *Meletē* does, however, apply indifferently to exercises in the other two branches of rhetoric, the forensic and the deliberative. Seneca's sharp division into *controversiae* and *suasoriae* is not stressed by the Greek teachers. They find a place for deliberative speeches in the *stasis*-system devised for classifying forensic cases, and they prefer to subdivide them, if they have to, into the historical and the fictitious (*plasmata*).³⁵

The second limitation is more important. The *meletē*, as a complete speech, is a more advanced exercise than the *progymnasmata*, the earlier stages of instruction in which the pupil was taught to compose what might become elements in the final

³³ Note also certain uses of the verb μελετᾶν: (i) 'to take the part of', e.g. μελετῶμεν τὸν Πάτροκλον (Choricius 38, init.); (ii) 'to deliver' a speech, e.g. Δημοσθένης τὸν ⟨περὶ⟩ παραπρεσβείας μελετῶν (*RG* IV.76.30); (iii) 'rehearse', e.g. Chariton 5.5.6, where Dionysius, about to appear in court, gets up early ἵνα μελετήσῃ τὴν δίκην.

³⁴ Menander Rhetor 331.16 Sp.: ἃς γὰρ ἐπιδείξεις λόγων πολιτικῶν οἱ σοφισταὶ καλούμενοι ποιοῦνται μελέτην ἀγώνων εἶναί φαμεν, οὐκ ἐπίδειξιν. ('The demonstrations of public speeches composed by the people known as sophists I regard as practice for real cases, not as true epideictic.')

³⁵ Deliberative speeches fall under *stasis pragmatikē* (below, p. 63). Hermogenes' rival, Minucianus (*RG* IV.181), proposed a division of subjects into *panēgyrika*, *dikanika*, *ēthika*, *pathētika*, *mikta* (i.e. epideictic or encomiastic, forensic, character-subjects, emotional, mixed), using what we may call the dominant tone of the piece as the basis of classification. For the division into imaginary and historical themes, see (e.g.) Philostratus, *VS* 481 (below n. 77).

product – narratives, descriptions, comparisons, *loci communes*, and so on.[36] The connection between 'parts' and 'whole' is obvious enough, and is sometimes made explicit. Thus Sopatros,[37] advising on an epilogue for a speech on behalf of a woman who has murdered her unfaithful husband, adds: 'you have got all the topics to fit in from the *progymnasma*'. We often observe *loci communes* and *theses* in declamation: the power of love,[38] the happiness of animals,[39] the divinity of Nature,[40] the variety of human pursuits[41] and national characteristics.[42] There are descriptions also: a battle,[43] a beauty,[44] a vivid scene.[45] But the most important of the *progymnasmata* was naturally the one that approached most nearly to the *meletē* itself. This was *ēthopoiia*, 'representation of character'. In this, the pupil was called upon to say 'what words' a given historical, mythological or purely imaginary character 'might speak' in certain circumstances. This, like the other *progymnasmata*, had its uses as an element in a speech. We often find declaimers, like real orators, lending vividness to their story by putting part of it into direct speech – the advice given by the father or received by the son, a husband's conversation with an estranged wife, or somebody's reflections on the turn of events.[46] The more of this there is, the greater the opportunities for variety and dramatic expression. But *ēthopoiia* was in itself half-way to *meletē*, and we need to know a little more about it. Usually, it had a mythical or historical setting, less often a purely general one: what would Menelaus say when Helen was taken from him, or Hector in Hades when he hears that Priam has taken food with Achilles, or the exiled Aeschines when Demosthenes offers him money, or the painter who falls in love with his own picture of a woman?[47] This sort of dramatic monologue is of course very like much poetical

---

[36] See D. L. Clark (1957), Kennedy (1983) 54–73.
[37] *RG* VIII.249.21.
[38] Liban. *Decl.* 7.8, 8.17, 8.23.
[39] Ibid. 12.6, 30.8.
[40] Ibid. 13.30.
[41] Ibid. 29.5, 31.29.
[42] Ibid. 13.3.
[43] Ibid. 37.8.
[44] Ibid. 12.26 (Alcibiades).
[45] Ibid. 5.26 (the removal of Briseis from Achilles' tent).
[46] E.g. Liban. *Decl.* 9.7–10; Sopatros, *RG* VIII.252.
[47] Severus, *RG* I.534ff.

composition: there were verse *ēthopoiiai*, often with Homeric themes;[48] and Ovid's *Heroides* show what the exercise might become in a poet's hands. *Ēthopoiia* was a very enduring form; it lasted in Greek rhetorical education longer than the full *meletē*, and we find many Byzantine examples which have Christian themes (a great rarity with *meletai* proper[49]): Nicephorus Basilakes[50] has Samson blinded, David and Saul, David and Absalom, Joseph in prison, Peter before the crucifixion, and the Virgin Mary commenting on Christ's first miracle at Cana; yet he also has frankly pagan themes, Atalanta in the race and Eros beholding a woodcutter poised to cut down Myrrha, who is pregnant with Adonis. The essential difference between *ēthopoiia* and *meletē* is that the former has no 'question' (*zētēma*); this means it has no legal setting and pleads no case. When we compose a speech for Aeschines 'on discovering a statue of Philip in Demosthenes' house', it is an *ēthopoiia*; when we imagine Demosthenes as tried for treason as a result of the discovery, and write speeches for defence and prosecution, it is *meletē*.[51]

4

The double rôle of the *meletē*, as practical exercise and as imaginative literature, means that its history is one of conflict between two opposing tendencies.

As an exercise, it was the crown of the curriculum, the pupil's and the teacher's chance to show what they could do, at least in a mock battle. We must not underestimate the practical side just because there is less evidence for it than for the literary and social aspects of the art. Sophists regularly engaged in real cases. Philostratus testifies to their legal, forensic and diplomatic activity. Herodes Atticus defends himself on a charge of causing the death of his wife Regilla, who was beaten when pregnant.[52]

[48] *Anth. Pal.* 9.453–80.
[49] A solitary Christian *meletē*, on Athanasius' fight for orthodoxy, is referred to in *RG* VI.542.10.
[50] *RG* I.466. This is twelfth-century work (Hunger [1978] 93ff; Kennedy [1983] 316).
[51] The *ēthopoiia* is in Severus (*RG* I.539), the *meletē* theme in Planudes (*RG* V.242); cf Kohl (1915) 67 (nos. 261–2).
[52] *VS* 555.

Nicetes 'was more powerful as an advocate than as a declaimer'.[53] Scopelianus takes up the cause of the wine-growers of Asia, and is himself involved in litigation with his father's cook, who had insinuated himself into the position of heir by persuading the old man that his son was going to poison him.[54] Aristides himself practised in court – though he says himself that his appearance on his own behalf was 'more like a display than a court matter'.[55] Actual speeches for named litigants are attested: Stobaeus gives us, for example, Gaius 'for Lucilla', 'against Menandra' and 'against Artemisios'; Obrimos 'for Protogonos on a charge of poisoning' and 'for Severus'; and Theodorus 'for Elpidephoriane'.[56] Dates and persons are unknown. If the cases are bizarre or scandalous, truth may yet be as strange as the declaimers' fictions. Libanius' pupils, too, expected to practise: Priscion, for instance, is both a teacher and an advocate.[57] Even the theorist Sopatros, in a discussion of Hermogenes' doctrine of the topics of 'will' and 'means', an arid and technical matter, makes it clear that what he is saying applies both 'in problems (zētēmata), and in everyday business'.[58]

This said, the absurdity of much of the game is evident. The fictions were often remote from real life, however bizarre that might be, and it was impossible to create in school the tensions of the court, the real emotions, the smell of guilt and deceit. Not unnaturally, many ancient critics denounced the whole thing as a fraud. This became a commonplace, especially in Roman

[53] VS 516.
[54] VS 516–17, 520. In general, see Bowie (1982) and Bowersock (1969) 56.
[55] Or. 50.88ff.
[56] Stobaeus 4.22.200, 4.22.201, 4.26.28, 4.5.69, 4.5.101, 4.22.117. The extracts are commonplaces (to suit Stobaeus' moral purposes) but some sound very declamatory. Thus 'Gaius for Paulus who killed his son while mad' (4.40.22): ἕστηκέ σοι παιδοφόνος πατήρ, τὴν μὲν χεῖρα μιαρώτατος τὴν δὲ ψυχὴν καθαρώτατος, μανίᾳ διακονησάμενος τὴν συμφοράν. ('There stands before you a father child-murderer, in hand most foul, in mind most pure, by his madness the instrument of his ruin.') Here the singular pronoun σοι suggests (though it does not prove) that the case is before a single magistrate, not the jury regular in declamations.
[57] Liban. Epist. 989.
[58] RG IV.185.3. Cf also ps.-Dionysius, Ars 371.23, for the contrast between σοφιστῶν διατριβαί ('sophists' classes') and πρὸς ἀλήθειαν ῥητορεύειν ('practising rhetoric in real life').

literature,[59] but also in Greek. The rhetors, of course, persisted. Abused by philosophers, ridiculed by practical men, a favourite butt of satirists, they went on displaying their art and advertising its virtues. It was, they claimed, the best way to train 'invention' — that is to say, to teach people how to think up relevant arguments and deploy them in the most effective way, having regard to the prejudices of the audience as well as the facts of the case. Ingenuity and organization were paramount.

But there was a feature of *meletē* present in school practice but even more important in the literary development of the form, which ran counter to this concern with argumentation: these speeches were always impersonations. The declaimer never appears in his own person, but always as some historical character or stock type. He becomes Themistocles or Alcibiades, Honest Poor Man or Old Miser. Less often, he becomes an advocate (*synēgoros*), a comparatively colourless rôle, only adopted when the circumstances demand it. Women usually need advocates, as they could not appear in court; but this rule is sometimes broken, as in the case of the mother who has killed her prostitute son in the gymnasium, whither he had fled for sanctuary because women were not allowed in.[60] Another special case is the rhetor who has had his tongue cut out;[61] and the question whether a convicted offender whose sentence is still at issue needs an advocate is debated at some length by a teacher who adduces Demosthenic parallels and finally decides to let the poor man speak for himself.[62] 'Advocates' are thus exceptional; as a rule

---

[59] See Bonner (1949) ch. 4, Bornecque (1902), Winterbottom (1980) 1–8. Passages of special interest are Petronius 1–4, Tacitus, *Dialogus* 35, Sen. *Contr.* 3 praef., Persius 1.85, 3.44–7, Juvenal 10.166, 7.115. A Greek instance (Synesius, *De insomniis* 20) is discussed below (p. 21).

[60] *RG* VIII.344. But a woman who has killed her unfaithful husband is represented by an advocate, *RG* VIII.247. Circumstances in which a *synēgoros* is needed are listed in [Hermogenes] *Peri Methodou Deinotētos* p. 436 Rabe. They are (1) for a woman; (2) for a child, aged person or sick man; (3) for a slave or person without rights; (4) in cases of indecency (specifically, homosexual prostitution).

[61] Liban. *Decl.* 36.

[62] [Liban.] *Decl.* 45, *protheōria*. The references to Demosthenes are to *Or.* 21. (*in Midiam*) 95, and *Or.* 57. (*in Eubulidem*) 6, 56.

the declaimer plays a part and displays a strong and distinctive *ēthos*. Now this might be not bad practice for an Attic speech-writer of the classical period, who needed to give his client words and thoughts not too inappropriate to his age and status;[63] but for most of the pupils who practised declamation through the Hellenistic and Roman period, it had no practical relevance at all. What it did do was to strengthen the tendency of the exercise to become literature, to turn it into a dramatic monologue with a plot. This development reaches its peak in Libanius, in whom *ēthos* predominates over everything else, and we get a corpus of speeches intended not only to amuse but to endure as literature.

5

This tendency of rhetoric to shift 'from discourse to literature' is an observable fact.[64] But it would be a gross over-simplification to say that the scholastic *meletē* preceded the literary, or that the latter is simply a development or perversion of the former. That idea does not stand up to a little reflection on ancient education and literature in general. The function of education was never wholly practical; preservation of a literary tradition and inculcation of social and political virtues were in it from the first. And imaginative speech-writing obviously holds an important place in Greek literature of all periods.

So the roots of the *meletē* lie deep. In a long view, the prestige and the development are no surprise.

From its inception, Greek literature is much concerned with *mimēsis* of speech. Homer differs from most other heroic poetry in his liberal use of direct speech. This attracted the attention of the Greeks themselves: Plato saw it, and inferred that Homer was a dangerous mimetic deceiver; Aristotle saw it, and found it evidence of Homer's mastery of his craft.[65] The early historians followed Homer's example, Herodotus more closely than

[63] See in general the last two chapters – 'Client and consultant' and 'Orator, rhetorician and reader' – in Dover (1968).

[64] Kennedy (1980) 5: 'It has been a persistent characteristic of classical rhetoric...to shift its focus from persuasion to narration, from civic to personal contexts, and from discourse to literature, including poetry.'

[65] Pl. *Rep.* 2.392ff; Aristotle, *Poetics* 1460a.

Thucydides: 'words' as well as 'deeds' were essential to their narrative. In the contrived political orations of Thucydides we have something distinguishable from *meletē* by one feature only, albeit a vital one: the writer's knowledge of and adherence to, the truth of the situation as he understood it. And this is to say nothing of drama.

So when the systematic teaching of rhetoric began in the late fifth century, there was already an established tradition of making up speeches in character for a variety of literary purposes. Teachers developing their techniques did not have to depend solely on the practice of the courts and assemblies. They were of course influenced by the democratic institutions, and especially by the Athenian system of large juries and litigants pleading in person. The size of the juries encouraged emotional appeals, the litigant required a speech to be composed for him appropriate to his known or visible character. But the teachers could draw themes and models from epic, drama or history and this made their teaching more amusing, less controversial and less banausic. A two-way traffic between the schools and the stage, for example, is already recognizable in the age of Euripides and Aristophanes.[66]

In these circumstances, it is not surprising that a good deal of imaginary oratory should be composed, quite apart from the historians' speeches. Some of it was pamphleteering, like much of Isocrates' work, or the various 'Accusations' and 'Defences' of Socrates. The prose encomium,[67] both serious and paradoxical, was born about the same time, and, though it is 'epideictic' and so not strictly within the tradition we are considering, it is not always easy to draw the line between it and the forensic and deliberative pieces which are properly the ancestors of later *meletē*. These include the mythological declamations of Gorgias – *Palamedes* and the more 'epideictic' *Helen* – which set an enduring fashion, the *Ajax* and *Odysseus* of Antisthenes, the speech

---

[66] 'Rhetorical' elements in tragedy have been much discussed; see, e.g., the indications and references in Kennedy (1963) ch. 2.

[67] On encomium, see Russell and Wilson, ed. of *Menander Rhetor*, pp. xiiiff, with the references there.

preserved as Oration IV of Andocides, and the speech in Plato's *Phaedrus* in which Lysias is shown discussing whether a lover or a non-lover should be 'gratified' by the young and beautiful.[68] We hear too of a 'defence of Nicias before his Syracusan captors' which Theophrastus said was by Lysias;[69] and a deliberative exercise in which advice is given for and against going to war on behalf of the Syracusans.[70] But the most important of these pieces, and probably the earliest, is the set of *Tetralogies* by Antiphon.[71] These have a distinctive feature which links them to the *meletē* as we know it in later times. Each set of little speeches deals with a different type of issue. The first is concerned with a question of fact: a man has been found dead, and his rich enemy is accused of his murder. The second is about a question of responsibility: was the boy who got in the way of the javelin and was killed more to blame for the accident than the thrower? The third deals with justifying a deliberate killing, and putting the blame elsewhere. These themes prefigure the later differences of *stasis* or 'issue';[72] and it was precisely to illustrate such differences that declamation themes were developed and classified.

Thus the ground for the growth of declamation was well prepared by the conditions of classical literature and rhetoric. Indeed, the fourth century may have produced much more that could almost be called declamation than we can safely assert. It is always possible that the corpus of the orators, as we have it, contains speeches so remote from actual occasions that they ought really to be treated as exercises.[73] But at some stage there took place a decisive change which marks the real beginning of the school tradition as the bulk of our evidence presents it. This is

[68] Andocides, *Or.* 4: Dover (1968) 191f. Lysias in *Phaedrus*: e.g. G. J. de Vries (1969) 11–14, for a recent statement of various views.

[69] Lysias fr. 71; Dover (1968) 98.

[70] *Rhetorica ad Alexandrum* 29.2.

[71] The most recent and informative edition is that of Caizzi (1969); see also Kennedy (1963) 129ff.

[72] So the ancient argument (*hypothesis*) to the *Tetralogies* alleges that I is a *stochasmos* (issue of fact), II *antenklēma* (counter-charge) or *metastasis* (transference), and III the same as II.

[73] Dover (1968) ch. 9, raises disquieting suspicions of this kind.

the introduction of certain stock themes – especially tyrannicide, rewards for valour, and adultery. It has been suggested that this may be quite early, and originate in Ionia in the fifth century rather than Athens in the fourth.[74] The grounds for believing this are the Ionic legal terms in Antiphon[75] and the importance of tyranny in Ionian history. But tyrants continued to be a problem right down to Roman times, and the impact of Athenian law and oratory must surely have been decisive. A date in the late fourth century seems more likely; and this was the view taken in antiquity by Quintilian[76] and by Philostratus,[77] both of whom were well placed to make informed guesses. Quintilian cautiously remarks that 'subjects invented in imitation of the law-courts and of deliberations' were introduced 'around (*circa*) Demetrius of Phalerum', though there was no sufficient evidence that Demetrius was himself concerned. Now Demetrius was a notorious historical turning-point, the orator whose easy elegance was seen, both by Cicero and by Quintilian, as marking the end of the great age and the onset of decadence.[78] But what does *circa* mean? Is

[74] Fairweather (1981) 114–15.
[75] On Antiphon's vocabulary, see Dover, *CQ* XLIV (1950) 44ff.
[76] Quint. 2.4.41: nam fictas ad imitationem fori consiliorumque materias apud Graecos dicere circa Demetrium Phalerea institutum fere constat. An ab ipso id genus exercitationis sit inventum, ut alio quoque libro sum confessus, parum comperi; sed ne ii quidem qui hoc fortissime adfirmant ullo satis idoneo auctore nituntur. ('It is generally agreed that speaking on themes invented in imitation of courts of law and public councils was a practice instituted among the Greeks around Demetrius of Phalerum. Whether this type of exercise was invented by Demetrius himself, I have been unable to ascertain with certainty, as I confessed also in another book [i.e. the lost *De causis corruptae eloquentiae*]; but even those who assert it most forcibly have no adequate authority to rely on.')
[77] Philostratus, *VS* 481: ἡ δὲ μετ' ἐκείνην [sc. σοφιστική], ἣν οὐχὶ νέαν – ἀρχαία γάρ – δευτέραν δὲ μᾶλλον προσρητέον, τοὺς πένητας ὑπετυπώσατο καὶ τοὺς πλουσίους καὶ τοὺς ἀριστέας καὶ τοὺς τυράννους καὶ τὰς ἐς ὄνομα ὑποθέσεις ἐφ' ἃς ἡ ἱστορία ἄγει. ἦρξε δὲ... Αἰσχίνης ὁ Ἀτρομήτου τῶν μὲν Ἀθήνησι πολιτικῶν ἐκπεσών, Καρίᾳ δὲ ἐνομιλήσας καὶ Ῥόδῳ. ('The "sophistic" after this, which should be called "second" rather than "new", for it is ancient, drew the outlines of the Poor Men and Rich Men, War Heroes and Tyrants, and also the named subjects which we derive from history. This was begun by...Aeschines the son of Atrometos, when he was exiled from Athenian public life and settled in Caria and Rhodes.')
[78] On Demetrius of Phalerum, see esp. Cic. *Orator* 92, 96, *Brutus* 37ff; Quint. 10.1.80. The tradition has been critically examined by K. Heldmann (1982)

Evidence, definitions, origins

it 'around the time of' or 'in the circle of'? If Quintilian had a Greek source which said οἱ περὶ (or ἀμφὶ) Δημήτριον, it might even have meant Demetrius himself.⁷⁹ Ambiguity remains. Philostratus' evidence is more explicit than that of Quintilian – but also more suspect, for Philostratus has an axe to grind. What he says comes at the beginning of his *Lives of the Sophists*, and its purpose is to advance an interpretation of literary history in which the great 'sophists' of the second and third centuries A.D. are seen as the inheritors of an ancient tradition. He distinguishes two 'sophistics'. One dealt with philosophical themes, moral and scientific; it was founded by Gorgias. The 'next sophistic' – 'not new but second, for it is ancient' – 'drew the outlines of the Poor Man and the Rich Man, the Heroes (*aristeis*) and the Tyrants, as well as the named subjects which we derive from history'. This 'second sophistic', says Philostratus, was founded by the orator Aeschines when he was exiled from Athens and taught rhetoric in Caria and Rhodes.⁸⁰ This was between 330 and 315 B.C. Date and place fit the phenomena quite well; and, whether or not Philostratus had any real evidence, there is no improbability in connecting these developments with the end of Athenian power and the dispersal of skilled teachers and orators to the eager audiences of a wider world.

Philostratus leaves out everything between Aeschines and Nicetes of Smyrna, who flourished under Nero. He drops a few names – Ariobarzanes, Xenophron, Peithagoras – but that is all. We can perhaps do a little better. Seneca's Greeks help to fill in the picture, and the papyri, as we have seen, make it clear that historical declamation was being written in the early Hellenistic period. The same inference follows from the cutting remarks of

---

99–122, who discusses Quint. 2.4.41 at length, though Philostratus does not come within his purview.

⁷⁹ Cf Kühner–Gerth, *Gr. Gramm.* 1.270, Arndt–Gingrich, *Lexicon of the New Testament*, s.v. περί; [Longin.] 13.3. We should, if we took this view, have to assume that Quintilian misunderstood his source.

⁸⁰ Aeschines' school in Rhodes ('Ροδιακὸν διδασκαλεῖον) was well known, and figures in the various ancient Lives; cf *Vita* 3 (Westermann, *Biographi Graeci Minores* 269). But accounts varied: some said he refused to teach a *technē* of rhetoric or to plead cases in court, but took up his father's trade as a schoolmaster.

Polybius,[81] when he criticizes the historian Timaeus for putting speeches into the mouths of his characters as though he was 'arguing a set case in a lesson' and following text-book rules like a schoolboy. Finally, there is the critic Demetrius: whatever his date, his examples reflect special knowledge of fourth- and third-century writing, and nothing later. So the few quotations that sound like declamation may tentatively be added here: the man who accuses Aristides of absence from the naval battle at Salamis; the man who said that 'Xerxes came down with all his people'; and the ingenious punster who bade King Alexander 'run his mother's name' – in other words, compete at Olympia, the name of which recalls that of his mother Olympias.[82]

Fragmentary and vague as our knowledge is, *meletē*, we may be sure, was familiar in the Hellenistic age.

[81] Polyb. 12.25a3, 8; 25k8. Fairweather (1981) 108.
[82] Demetrius 238 (cf Kohl [1915] 53), 187, 236. The date of Demetrius is uncertain. Grube (1961) 56 argues for 'Alexandria, not much later than 270 B.C.', but there is no convincing evidence for this. However, the amount of early (i.e. fourth- and early third-century) material in the book is considerable, and there is therefore a probability that these examples also are relatively early.

2
Sophistopolis, or the world of the Aristeus

Et ideo ego adulescentulos existimo in scholis stultissimos fieri quia nihil ex his quae in usu habemus aut audiunt aut vident.

'The reason why young men become such idiots in school is, I think, that they neither hear nor see any of the things of our ordinary life.'

Petronius

I

Synesius' treatise *On Dreams*, written 'in a single night' in A.D. 403 or 404, contains an entertaining satire on declaimers at work:

It seems to me that it is inappropriate to exercise one's skill on Miltiades and Cimon and an assortment of anonymous characters, or on the political enmities of Rich Man and Poor Man, over which I saw two elderly gentlemen disputing in the public theatre. Both of them were very serious about their philosophy, and each carried, by my estimate, a talent's weight of beard. But all this seriousness didn't stop them from abusing one another and waxing indignant, waving their arms about uncontrollably in the process of delivering lengthy speeches on behalf of – well, at the time I thought it was friends of theirs, but actually, as people lost no time in pointing out to me, it was persons who, far from being their friends, never existed then, or earlier, or indeed in the natural world at all. For where can there be a form of government that allows the war hero as his reward the right to kill a fellow citizen who is his political rival? And when a man of ninety debates a fiction, how long is he putting off study of the truth?[1]

Synesius, as the last sentence shows, speaks as a philosopher, for whom rhetoric is a frivolous hindrance to salvation. The ninety-year-old is Libanius, who was born in 314. The subject was identified by Synesius' commentator[2] as one in which a rich man promises to supply food to the citizens if he is allowed to

[1] Synesius, *De insomniis* 20, pp. 187–8 Terzaghi.
[2] Nicephorus Gregoras: see Foerster's ed. of Libanius, VII.183 n. 1.

kill his poor enemy; the agreement is made, but the rich man neglects to feed the poor man's children, and is accused of murder when they die.[3]

Where indeed do such things happen? Only in a city of the imagination, from which there is less to be learned about the realities of ancient life than about its characteristic fantasies. It is certainly possible to form a picture of this imaginary world; and this is, I think, both a legitimate and a useful exercise. In so far as declamation is an educational tool, the study of its settings gives an idea of the values and prejudices that teachers assumed or encouraged. In so far as it is literature, or at least 'sub-literature', its characteristic scenarios and attitudes have the same sort of interest as the world of the comic or the detective story – or, for that matter, the world of the epic. Let us at least make the attempt.

2

Let us call the imaginary city 'Sophistopolis'. It is of course a Greek city and worships Greek gods. Most important, it is (like classical Athens) a democracy, where the rhetor – both politician and expert in oratory[4] – is something of a hero. He persuades an enemy to make peace: does he deserve the war hero's privilege?[5] He is so successful that they forbid him to speak and he teaches instead: has he broken the ban?[6] His encomium on death causes an epidemic of suicide; is he to blame?[7] That democracy is the right form of government, no one ever doubts. Partisans of the *dēmos* are honest, the rich are cruel, potential tyrants are a constant danger. There is a popular assembly, easily moved to tears or anger and even to riot. There is a council (*boulē*) which has some judicial functions – in particular, it hears requests for leave to commit suicide. The executive authority is in the hands of a single general (*stratēgos*) or of a college of *stratēgoi* – not

---

[3] Cf Liban. *Decl.* 35 for the setting of this *plasma*.

[4] This ambiguity of ῥήτωρ is easily exploited. The word was used in fifth-century Athens of 'speakers' who proposed measures to the assembly; hence it often means 'politicians' and οἱ ῥήτορες in this sense incur comic abuse. The sense 'teacher of rhetoric' is later.

[5] Choricius, *Or.* 42.

[6] Anon., *RG* VIII.408.   [7] Ibid. VIII.407.

the Athenian ten, but some smaller number.⁸ And this divergence from Athenian practice is interesting. Even in a variant of the Arginusae story,⁹ there is a single general against whom the charge of abandoning the dead and wounded is brought. Now both in classical times and later there were many cities that had executive *stratēgoi*, single or collegiate; and the declaimers no doubt took this common situation, without troubling much about historical niceties.¹⁰ The point is that the arrangements known from the Attic orators and historians were not taken into the *mise-en-scène* of *plasmata*. Similarly with the judicial system: large jury-courts are not regularly assumed, and in one of the few places where details are given, we hear of a court of seven judges that divides two, two, three in assessing a penalty: do the three constitute a majority?¹¹

The primary function of the *stratēgos* is of course to lead in war. Sophistopolis is usually at war with her neighbours, and her young men conscripted for service. Illness grants exemption, but does love?¹² A father shows his boy the corpses, and the boy dies of shock: has the father caused his death?¹³ Yet for most of the time when the rhetors were composing and teaching these exercises, real Greek cities were locally at peace; the only wars that might affect them were conducted by the Roman power, either against barbarian enemies or when it was at loggerheads with itself. This is of course less true of the Hellenistic age, but the constant campaigning – with its individual heroism and cruel sieges – is hardly a reflection of any direct experience. War,

⁸ Single *stratēgos*: e.g. Liban. *Decl.* 44, Sopatros, *RG* VIII.198, 232. College: e.g. Apsines 267.6ff Sp.-H.

⁹ *P. Dugit* (Jander [1913] 63) = *RG* VIII.223 (Sopatros).

¹⁰ See in general W. Schwahn, *RE* VI.1081ff. Literary texts which bear on this include Acts 16.20, Chion, *Epist.* 13, Chariton 4.5.

¹¹ [Liban.] *Decl.* 45, cf *Decl.* 46. Dr Winterbottom draws my attention to [Quint.] *Decl. min.* 365, *RLM* 97.15–19 (Fortunatianus), Gellius 9.15.7. The problem of what constitutes a majority is also in Heliodorus 1.14.1, where the court is 2,700 strong, with 1,000 for exile and the rest divided between two different modes of execution.

¹² Sopatros, *RG* VIII.185. This may be added to the literary evidence for the topic of love's sickness adduced by C. Miralles, in *Erotica Antiqua*, ed. B. P. Reardon (Bangor 1976) 20f.

¹³ *RG* VIII.185 (Sopatros).

however, was essential to the declaimers' world. It was necessary to justify their favourite character, the *aristeus* (in Latin *vir fortis*[14]), the hero returning from the front to claim his reward.

Aristeus is a Homeric word,[15] and represents a very Homeric and Hellenic idea. From early times, Greek competitiveness displayed itself in emulation in battle: Homer's heroes aim 'to be best' (*aristeuein*) and have their individual days of glory (*aristeiai*), more important even than the fortunes of the war. This emphasis on individual prowess remained strong in historical times. Herodotus[16] records the *aristeia* of Archias of Samos, and relates how he was buried at public expense; the informant is the hero's grandson. Again, in the narratives of Thermopylae and Plataea, Herodotus is at pains to indicate *aristeiai*, while the competition for rewards after Salamis, in which Themistocles and Eurybiades were both honoured, was a particularly famous and influential story.[17] Famous too was the award of a crown and a panoply to Alcibiades for his valour at Potidaea.[18] The criteria for such awards were often discussed. Alcibiades himself, in Plato's *Symposium*,[19] alleges that it was Socrates who really deserved the prize at Potidaea, for without him he could not himself have got home safely. And this precise point – the relative claims of rescuer and rescued hero – is the subject of an interesting piece of Hellenistic rhetoric, the debate between Aristomenes and Cleonnis in Diodorus' narrative of the Messenian wars.[20] Yet of the one special feature of the *aristeus*' lot which most concerned the declaimers, his free choice of reward, there is no historical evidence at all. Its convenience for constructing moral and legal dilemmas is obvious; so is its likeness to the fairy-tale motif of giving people 'wishes' which their folly may turn to disaster. Some *aristeis* ask for other men's wives,[21] one

---

[14] This equivalence leads Plutarch (*Mor.* 319B) to give ἀριστευτικός as one interpretation of the Latin *fortis*.

[15] Plutarch (*Mor.* 156E, 706E) uses it to mean 'Homeric hero' as well as in the rhetors' special sense (as in *Mor.* 1126E).

[16] Herodotus 3.55.

[17] Herodotus 7.73, 7.226–7, 9.71.   [18] Isocrates, *Or.* 16.29–30.

[19] Pl. *Symp.* 219E. On Socrates as a soldier, see esp. Düring (1941) 41–6.

[20] Diodorus 8.10–12.   [21] *RG* VIII.402, 405.

for a Vestal Virgin.[22] One wants exiles restored and prisoners released, and is accordingly charged with aiming at tyranny,[23] another more humanely begs the life of his cowardly son.[24] Yet another involves himself in self-contradiction. After his first *aristeia*, he asks that his statue shall henceforth be an inviolable sanctuary. After his second, he asks for the death of a poor enemy, who naturally seeks sanctuary at the statue.[25] Sometimes – and this too is unhistorical – rival claims to the prize are settled by a duel.[26] A father and two sons all distinguished themselves, and all have a claim. One son then kills the other, but concedes the prize to his father without a contest, though the father insists on fighting. In a variant, the brothers fight and the sun is darkened: the portent suggests divine displeasure, and it is proposed that the law should be changed. Or they fight, and the elder is killed; the victor then asks as his reward that his deed shall never be recorded in a picture or statue.

So war is perpetual. Sometimes the army marches out and there is room for heroism – always in defence, for Sophistopolis is never the aggressor – and at other times the city is under siege. This too sets problems. Resident foreigners are not allowed on the walls; one disobeys, and distinguishes himself in fighting off the besiegers. Should he be executed for his trespass or rewarded for services rendered? Cicero[27] reasonably calls this case puerile; but it seems never to have lost its attraction. Similar is the problem of the locked gate:[28] the law says the gate must never be opened at night, but friendly troops are caught outside and massacred, because nobody will let them in.[29] Often, it is a tyrant who lays siege to the city, and the circumstances dimly recall the tale of Troy – just as the duels between brothers dimly recall Polynices and Eteocles. In a theme which occurs in various forms, the tyrant is in love with a girl or boy in the city, and brings

[22] Ennodius, *Decl.* 223. [23] Liban. *Decl.* 37.
[24] Sopatros, *RG* VIII.306. [25] *RG* VIII.412.
[26] Bonner (1949) 88; Calp. Flacc. 21; Apsines 234.15 Sp.–H.; Hermogenes 98.20ff Rabe; Sopatros, *RG* VIII. 320.
[27] Cic. *De oratore* 2.100.
[28] *RG* IV.698, IV.246, VIII.411; Hermogenes 118 Rabe; Apsines 242 Sp.–H.
[29] See below, ch. 6, p. 121.

up his army to gratify his passion. The siege is desperate; and ultimately the parent of the young person is compelled to sacrifice his child on the walls, in full view of the besieger, who then withdraws frustrated.[30] In the most elaborate version of this, Choricius makes the girl's lover commit suicide after her death; his father then accuses her father of responsibility for the boy's fate. To make the story less psychologically implausible, Choricius gives the girl's father several children, so as not to make him willing to lose his only child.

'Pirates standing on the beach with chains' and 'oracles demanding the sacrifice of virgins to avert pestilence' are among the themes that Petronius[31] lists as typical absurdities of the genre. The Greek tradition provides examples of these perils too, though the classic pirate stories are in Seneca,[32] and it may be right to associate them with the prevalence of piracy in the Hellenistic world.[33] A wife goes to ransom her husband from pirates, but is drowned; the husband comes home, is ordered by his father to marry again, refuses and is disowned.[34] A father and daughter are kidnapped, and the father offers her hand to any ransomer; a man takes up the offer, finds the father dead, and ransoms the girl; when they get home, her kinsman claims her, not admitting the validity of the father's offer.[35] The 'sacrifice' stories are sometimes very sensational. A general is sent to consult the oracle at Delphi about how to bring a plague to an end. He is told that his son must be sacrificed. He conceals this; but the boy finds out and kills himself. The plague ceases, and the general is charged with dishonest dealing.[36] On another occasion,[37] a sorcerer's daughter[38] is chosen for sacrifice to abate the plague, and he

[30] A boy is the victim in Calp. Flacc. 39 and Liban. *Decl.* 42, a girl in Choricius, *Or.* 35 (= *Decl.* 9).
[31] Petronius, *Satyricon* 1–2.
[32] *Contr.* 1.6, 7.1.
[33] So Kennedy (1972) 334; but the theme also occurs in the *Odyssey*, and this alone may account for its persistent popularity.
[34] Liban. *Decl.* 46.   [35] *RG* VIII.365, cf 409.
[36] *RG* VIII.232.   [37] Liban. *Decl.* 41.
[38] The *magos* might seem an attractive character for sensational problems of the kind declaimers liked: cf Philostratus, *VS* 619, where a sorcerer seeks to die because he cannot kill a rival sorcerer who has seduced his wife. Magic in various

promises to stop it himself if they spare her – only to be asked, naturally enough, why he had not acted before, if he really had the power.

3

To these external perils, Sophistopolis added the wounds of its innumerable internal conflicts. The rich struggle with the poor, parents with children, husbands with wives.

In the Greek declaimers – and occasionally in the Roman[39] – the conflict between rich and poor is very much a political one. The contestants are political enemies. Morally speaking, it is a very one-sided conflict, in which the rich are always unjust and cruel and the poor are innocent victims. 'Let us poor men found our own city, for the rich have got theirs' says a speaker invented by Hermagoras and reported by Seneca.[40] 'Everyone who has suppressed democracy has done so by means of wealth', says the accuser of a wealthy adulterer in Libanius.[41] Only grudgingly is it admitted that some rich men can accommodate themselves to a democratic régime.[42] This attitude may surprise. It is at variance with the philosophers' and historians' more aristocratic line, evident in Plato, Theopompus or Plutarch, where a measure of hostile criticism towards the classical Athenian *dēmos* is always present. It is also at odds with the fact that the teaching of rhetoric was in real life directed at the well-to-do; the sophists of the great period were themselves men of substance, surely bound to share the interests and feelings of the rich and powerful. Why then should they so constantly press the lesson of the evils of wealth and the rights of the poor to justice? The motives were mixed. It was creditable to give moral warnings, and it helped to clear the rhetor from the philosopher's insistent charge that his art was immoral. Moreover, the fantasy of the underdog's victory is always potent; and to some degree the rhetor, because his power

forms is in fact a commoner theme in the literature of the Empire (Lucian, Apuleius, the novel) than it is in the declamations. The reason may be that it was not to any extent a theme of classical Attic literature, and the declaimers are generally bound by what they found there.

[39] Calp. Flacc. 7.
[40] Hermagoras in *Contr.* 10.15 (cf ch. 1, n. 30).
[41] Liban. *Decl.* 38.24.   [42] Liban. *Decl.* 35.7.

rested not on resources but on his personal skill, could represent himself as the voice of the oppressed.

All this is a striking simplification of the world. In Attic courts in the classical period there was naturally more realism.[43] Wealth gave advantages, and incurred odium; but its generous use diminished this, and it was generally not the possession of riches so much as the *hybris* of the rich – especially the self-made men – that earned disapproval. In the rhetors, no nuances remain. Everything is either black or white. We hear little of the generosity of the wealthy, and if the poor man sins his poverty is his best excuse. This is best shown by a case in Sopatros,[44] in which a young man is forbidden to speak in public because he has wasted his substance, although he has spent it entirely in the public service. His accusers say that this is no excuse: a bankrupt is a bankrupt, however his failure happened; and the young man's patriotic generosity is little but a show, a cover, in all probability, for evil living.

The wickedness of the rich appears on every hand. Pirates kidnap the son of a poor demagogue. A rich man, his political adversary, is sent to deal with the pirates. The boy is thrown overboard by his captors, and the general, instead of picking him up, concentrates on seizing the pirate ship. On his return home, he is prosecuted for abandoning the boy.[45]

A rich man promises to defeat the enemy if his poor rival's tongue is cut out. It is done, and the war is won. The poor man weeps in the assembly, and so stirs the crowd that they stone the rich man to death. He is charged with causing a civil disturbance. The defence represents the war as entirely a stratagem of the rich man, who was in collusion with the enemy; the stoning was 'constitutionally appropriate'.[46]

---

[43] Süss (1910) 235; note esp. Isaeus, *Or.* 5, Hyperides, *Or.* 3.
[44] *RG* VIII.356ff.
[45] Apsines 241 Sp.–H.
[46] Liban. *Decl.* 36. For the notion of 'weeping' as an expression of feeling where words are impossible, cf *RG* IV.469, where an *atimos* ('disfranchised', so deprived of the right of public speech and as good as dumb) finds his wife seduced, weeps, and thereby incites the *dēmos* to stone the adulterer; the consequence is that he is charged with causing a public disturbance (δημοκοπίου). (For the charge,

A rich man goes to dinner in a poor man's house. His host's pretty daughter waits at table. The rich man asks if she is a slave or a free woman. The father is ashamed, and says she is a slave. The guest rapes her. The law is that the penalty for the rape of a free woman is death, for that of a slave a fine of 100 talents. The rich man offers the money; the poor man demands his death.[47]

A rich *aristeus* asks for a poor man's daughter in marriage. She hangs herself rather than agree. He asks for another daughter — still as his hero's reward. The poor man opposes him.[48]

A poor man is condemned to death, and handed over to the executioner. The rich man buys him from the executioner for a talent and kills him himself for pleasure. He is accused of murder.[49]

A poor man is attacked in the street. Before he dies, he states that his attacker had a burnt face. The rich man's house has been on fire; he is found with a burnt face, and accused of the assault.[50]

Perhaps the most striking of these 'rich man, poor man' stories is one sensationally written up by Himerius.[51] Like other themes, this has affinities with myth, this time with the legend of Oedipus. Poor Man — politically active, of course — has exposed his infant son, because he cannot afford to bring him up. Rich Man, childless and anxious for an heir, has taken in the foundling and brought him up as his own son. The boy grows up in affluence, with the will and the means to satisfy his desires. Encouraged by his supposed father, he seduces Poor Man's wife, not knowing that she is his own mother. Poor Man catches the couple in bed, and runs his sword through the pair of them. Rich Man then appears, carrying the tokens (*gnōrismata*) which he had found with the infant. He discloses the child's true parentage, which he had known all the time. The closing part of the speech makes the Poor Man, who is prosecuting the rich villain for being responsible for

cf Sen. *Contr.* 3.8, where a weeping father incites a crowd to burn down a house where his son has been raped: a Greek theme, set, like many, after the capture of Olynthus.)

[47] *RG* VIII. 408, cf *Decl. min.* 301.
[48] *RG* VIII.339.
[49] *RG* IV.189.
[50] *RG* VIII.50.
[51] Himerius, *Or.* 4 Colonna.

the deaths, imagine a series of paintings in which the whole dreadful story is illustrated. The *ekphrasis* does duty as peroration:

> Let the paints come from the meadows of Vengeance and the Furies, let the tablet be made of some accursed and unholy wood, let the fire which ministers to the painting be that which the demons who avenge such deaths are wont to kindle. Look for a painter tragic in hand, and yet more tragic in mind. Bid him make a series of pictures out of the series of my misfortunes, but paint no event earlier than the exposure of the child. He must not show me speaking in public, addressing the people, wearing a garland, fortunate beyond others; let his whole painting be filled with my more grievous destiny. Let there be, first, the unhappy father, carrying the child in his arms into the desert, lamenting his fortune, weeping for the loss, repeatedly turning back, laying down the child and picking it up again, yielding to nature, then beaten by necessity. If he can, let the painting also represent the words, by the grimness of the face; let everyone hear what is said from the expression. Next, please, depict that marvellous love affair. Or rather, do not tell lies about my son. Make him hesitant, always procrastinating, going forward and then backing off, dazzled in mind but driven by fear, terrified of adultery, but not yet knowing that he is being forced to act against his own mother.
>
> Then paint the poor old lady: in love, but wrinkled and grey, so that the strangeness of the drama can be made all the more striking. And then come to the crowning episode of all: arm the poor man in his misery against those dearest to him, represent every particular whose semblance may sate your inhumanity. Set down the last scene too: *you*, showing yourself before the corpses with the tokens, smiling, cheerful, delighted with what has happened. But reserve a part of the picture for me, lest someone asks 'Where is he? Where is the unfortunate poor man? How did he stay alive? How did he survive such disasters?' Yet you shall not be happy in all things, man of wealth. You too must be a part of the play. In every lofty tragedy we know, tyrants are laid low.

4

Choricius observes that, as declamation can mimic any real case, it admits disputes between parents and children.[52] He perhaps says this to disarm the families of prospective pupils, for rhetors had always to be on their guard against the charge that their

---

[52] *Decl.* 5, p. 225 F–R (cf below, p. 103).

teaching was subversive. A deeper analysis may suggest that the schoolmaster's concern with parent–children conflicts had some sort of cathartic effect.[53] In any case, such conflicts, even disastrous ones, were commonplace in Greek legend and literature: we see them among the gods, in tragedy – Creon and Haemon in the *Antigone* – and in comedy, both Old and New. So it is no wonder they abound in declamation also.

Sympathy is usually with the children. Parents sometimes act with great barbarity: a father kills his daughter and her husband in order to recover the dowry.[54] But the typical parental act is an unjust or disputable 'disowning' (*apokēryxis*, Latin *abdicatio*). This theme has no doubt a background in real life.[55] In Athenian law, a father had the right to revoke his original acceptance of the child. The consequences of this were serious, for the child lost not only his right of inheritance but his place in the family. *Abdicatio*, on the other hand, seems to correspond to no precise procedure in Roman law; it is, says Bonner, 'more in the nature of a moral repudiation'. Quintilian[56] indicates that the school arguments about it were more or less those that might arise in real life in cases of challenging unfair exclusions from inheritance. The declaimers no doubt felt free to invent much; both the consequences and the justification of the act of 'disowning' could be varied at pleasure. We are told, for example, that the 'disowned' son had no share in his father's property,[57] and that he was so cut off from the family that it was an offence for him to mourn at his father's grave.[58] As to causes, one late rhetor instances love (for which the young man can only plead to be forgiven), persistent absence from home, being discovered at the frontier with a sword, and madness.[59] Dissolute life was obviously thought a prime cause: Libanius[60] makes fun of rhetors who teach young men to plead that they are neither lecherous nor spendthrift and haunt no brothel or gambling-den. But many teachers amused themselves and their pupils by inventing all sorts

---

[53] Kennedy, *ARRW*, 334–5.
[54] Liban. *Decl.* 40.
[55] Bonner (1949), 109; Harrison (1968) 76ff.
[56] Quint. 7.4.11.
[57] Hermogenes 41 Rabe.
[58] *RG* VIII.124.
[59] *RG* VIII.394.
[60] *Decl.* 27.10.

of variations designed to produce the maximum clash of personality between old and young. One son cohabits with his father's mistress,[61] another becomes a prostitute;[62] a farmer disowns a boy who takes up philosophy,[63] a miser does it because his son has idiotically chosen a crown of wild olive[64] – as recommended by Plato[65] – as his reward for heroism in battle; for the misanthrope (*dyskolos*)[66] it is enough that his son laughs at him when he falls down.

Small wonder, then, that the 'disowned' in Sophistopolis formed a large disaffected group. The private disputes of families spilled over into public affairs, and furnished the material of revolution and especially of tyranny. That the situation should be conceived like this was nothing new. Plato's imaginative psychology of changing constitutions makes a connection between the licence and rebellion of children and changes in public life. Sallust links the disaffection of rich and dissolute young men with the accretion of support to the subversive conspiracy of Catiline. But in the society of the declamations, where everything is seen very personally, the links between private and public action are particularly clear. We are bound to ask whether the declaimers' obsession with tyrants and tyrannicide has any basis in the politics of their own time, or is simply a melodramatic element in their historical fiction. The latter view is often taken; but in fact, local tyrannies were as liable to arise in Hellenistic and even Roman times as in the classical period. Tyranny was not a special phenomenon of a particular phase in Greek history, but something always likely to recur. Roman civil wars often encouraged local despots, favoured by one side or the other. Nicias, tyrant of Cos in Cicero's time, and overthrown under Octavian, is a good example; Antony's tyrant supporters include Strato at Amisus and Adiatorix at Heraclea.[67] It was no fantasy danger, however fantastic some of the details. Prosecutions for 'aiming at tyranny'

---

[61] *RG* VIII.78. Cf Aelian, *Epist. rust.* 19 for a similar theme outside *meletē*, though in a related genre: a father disowns his son for marrying a flute-girl.
[62] *RG* IV.96.
[63] Hermogenes 38 Rabe.
[64] Liban. *Decl.* 33; see below, p. 96ff.
[65] Plato, *Laws* 12.943.
[66] Liban. *Decl.* 26; see below, p. 89.
[67] Bowersock (1965) 45.

(*epithesis tyrannidos*) are conducted in Sophistopolis on a great many different grounds. Securing a bodyguard[68] and storing arms[69] were obvious evidence; promising prisoners freedom,[70] supporting the 'disowned',[71] or using your privilege as *aristeus* to restore exiles or the disfranchised[72] were hardly less common. Other signs of evil intent seem less substantial; the young man who looks up at the acropolis with tears in his eyes was a much favoured character.[73] As tyrants were suppressed, so tyrannicides were rewarded: a rich theme, useful to Cicero in *Pro Milone* and in the *Philippics*. Like *aristeis*, they were sometimes allowed, quite unhistorically, to choose their own reward. They could also dispute the prize; the instigator of the deed and the person who accidentally does what someone else had planned could both put in their claim.[74] Two doctors dispute it, because one treated the tyrant with a poisonous drug and the other gave the antidote: from which did he really die?[75]

5

The domestic life of Sophistopolis is as turbulent as its public affairs. Failure to marry – as in Sparta and in Plato's Cretan utopia[76] – is an offence: witness the ten young men accused of 'evil living' because they pledge themselves to a bachelor life.[77] But marriage and family bring many troubles. Adultery is common, and unfaithful wives and their lovers may legitimately be killed 'in the act'. Dowries are given, and may be kept by the husband if the wife is unfaithful to him. Rapists are offered the choice between death and marriage with their victim, though they are often let off with a fine.

Now all this has some basis in legal reality. It was indeed legitimate for husbands to kill adulterers, both under Attic law

[68] *RG* VIII.1ff; see below, ch. 6, p. 123.
[69] Liban. *Decl.* 37.
[70] Hermogenes 49 Rabe.
[71] Ibid. 47.
[72] Liban. *Decl.* 37.
[73] Hermogenes 49 Rabe, Apsines 243.12 Sp.–H.
[74] *RG* VIII.98.
[75] *RG* VIII.403.
[76] *Dikē agamiou*: Plutarch, *Lycurgus* 15, Pl. *Laws* 6.774.
[77] Apsines 223.24; 276.14 Sp.–H.; Hermogenes 44 Rabe.

and, in certain circumstances, under Roman.[78] Demosthenes and Lysias provided literary evidence for classical Athens. Roman law allowed the husband to keep at least a proportion of the dowry in case of adultery. The 'rapist's choice', on the other hand, seems to be more or less a fiction; at least the evidence for it, apart from declamation, is in comedy.[79] We should therefore not expect too close adherence to any particular code; here, as always, the declaimer sets his problem by saying 'let there be a law' (*nomos estō*), not by saying what the law actually is.[80] And it is of course his business to invent situations in which general, not legal, arguments can be advanced, and at the same time to make the whole thing as amusing as he can. So[81] a husband, having killed the adulterer, finds his wife weeping at the tomb – and so kills her as well, in contravention, it would seem, of a supposed law[82] which forbade the killing of the wife except *in flagrante delicto* with her lover. A woman is caught in adultery with her dead daughter's suitor, and is accused of poisoning the daughter.[83] A father commits adultery with his son's wife; another encourages his son to marry in order to get a woman in the house for himself.[84] A husband makes an assignation with his wife under a false name, then divorces her for adultery and keeps her dowry; the procedure pleases him, and he does it all over again with a new wife.[85] Similar legal unreality attaches to the other sexual

---

[78] Athens: Harrison (1968) 32f; see esp. Lysias, *Or.* 1, Demosth. *Or.* 59. Rome: *Digest* 48.5; *Codex* 9.9; Corbett (1969) 127ff; Bonner (1949) 120.

[79] Harrison (1968) 19; Bonner (1949) 89. Comic evidence includes Plautus, *Aulularia* 791, *Trinummus* 841, Terence, *Adelphoe* 724. Bonner's argument (loc. cit.) that the denial of 'rapist's choice' in the *Codex* implies that it was a fact of real life seems forced.

[80] Though later sophists might have legal knowledge, the professions of orator and lawyer were generally distinct. In classical Greece, there were no 'lawyers'; in Rome, *iuris consulti* were experts whom the advocate or the client could consult. Cicero sometimes (e.g. *Orator* 120) requires the orator to have some legal knowledge, but also (*De oratore* 1.234ff, esp. 250ff, in the speech of Antonius) makes the point that the orator/advocate should not bury himself in the law, but inquire what he needs in each case from the expert.

[81] Hermogenes 43 Rabe.

[82] Quintilian 7.1.7; cf *RG* VIII.252.

[83] Hermogenes 43 Rabe, Sen. *Contr.* 6.6.

[84] Liban. *Decl.* 38, 39.

[85] See below, p. 59.

Sophistopolis, or the world of the Aristeus 35

cases. A girl who is guiding her blind father is attacked, and the father falls to his death; the rapist offers a recognized fine, but the girl charges him with causing her father's death. This is a case of 'conflict of laws'.[86] Again, a general rapes a colleague's daughter, offers the fine but is accused of an offence against the state, on the ground that personal distress to an official affects the whole community.[87] We cannot draw any conclusions about real society from such things, nor, I think, from the fact that homosexual prostitution plays a considerable part in the rhetor's curriculum. The main reason for this will be the existence of a classical model, Aeschines' speech against Timarchus. But there are some bizarre cases. A boy threatens to become a prostitute unless he is provided with an adequate income by his family within thirty days. He receives a legacy, quite unexpectedly. He therefore does not carry out his threat; but none the less is debarred from speaking in public as a person of ill fame.[88] And the risk of being thought immoral in this way seems to have been an ever-present one: if a young man takes undue care with his appearance, he may well be charged with prostitution.[89]

6

So disturbed a world might well make suicide an attraction. One of the most striking scenarios of Sophistopolis is the *prosangelia* (προσαγγελία), the legal process in which a man 'denounces himself' to the Council, declares that his life is not worth living, and asks permission to put an end to it – usually by a dose of hemlock. Strange as this is (though 'permission to kill oneself' was, once, after all, familiar in Japanese society), it is alleged to have a basis in fact. Valerius Maximus[90] declares that it was the

---

[86] *RG* VIII.362, 370. See below p. 67, n. 76.
[87] *RG* VIII.105.
[88] *RG* IV.469. [89] Hermogenes 48 Rabe.
[90] Valerius Maximus 2.6.8; Foerster, Libanius VI.494, n. 1. The rhetor Albucius Silus (Suet. *Rhet.* 30) adapted the theme to his own real situation: convocata plebe causis, propter quas mori destinasset, diu ac more contionantis redditis, abstinuit cibo. For self-denunciation in another context, cf Ctesias, *FrGrHist* 688F9, where Astyages is said ἑαυτὸν προσαγγεῖλαι (to Cyrus) ἵνα μὴ δι' αὐτὸν στρεβλωθείησαν οἱ παῖδες.

law of Massilia that a citizen who proved to the satisfaction of the Council of Six Hundred that he wished to die – either because of misfortune or to avoid outliving good fortune – might be granted the hemlock. The custom, he says, is of Greek origin: he had himself witnessed it at Iulis in Ceos, when he was on his way to Asia with Sextus Pompeius;[91] a woman of high rank, ninety years old, successfully applied, and expired with dignity in the presence of the proconsul. This is so circumstantial that it is churlish to disbelieve, though one might interpret the event in various ways – for example, as ostentatious euthanasia, using the supposed law as scencry. The uses made of the idea by the declaimers are obviously fantastic. It was of course a very convenient notion, since it preserves a legal setting without requiring any legal contest. There are numerous examples in Sopatros, and Libanius is particularly fond of it. We have the misanthropist who cannot live with his talkative wife; the miser for whom it is intolerable to pay 1,000 drachmas in tax because he has unearthed buried treasure which is only worth half as much; and the parasite going out to dinner whose horse mistook the altar at his host's door for the turning point of a race-course, and so bolted home with his starving master on his back.[92] In Libanius, it is all comedy; the misanthropist and the parasite, after all, are standard comic characters. In Sopatros there is a somewhat different turn.[93] A heroic father asks for the life of a cowardly son, and obtains it; but he is rumoured to be having an affair with the son's wife, and the son, rather than accept his safety from his father, 'asks leave to die'. This, says Sopatros, is a 'figured problem' (*eschēmatismenon zētēma*),[94] because no one really wants to die when he can live, and the son's purpose in bringing the action is to denounce his father for breaking up his marriage. Similarly, for Sopatros, the miser who sells land on which the purchaser then discovers treasure 'denounces himself' with the

---

[91] Usually supposed to be the consul of A.D. 14, who was proconsul of Asia after A.D. 27; but this is not certain.

[92] Liban. *Decl.* 26, 28, 31 (and Sopatros, *RG* VIII.315ff).

[93] *RG* VIII.306ff.

[94] On this concept see esp. the two treatises περὶ ἐσχηματισμένων in [Dion. Hal.] *Ars rhetorica* (pp. 295–358 U.–R.). See above, ch. 1, n. 26.

real object of laying claim to what has been found; likewise the other miser who has paid a prostitute a talent, wants it back, and goes about it by declaring he cannot live. The concept of a speech which seems to have one purpose but in fact has another is an important one; in using the *prosangelia* themes to illustrate it, Sopatros points a lesson which could conceivably be useful in real life in a way that the straightforward character-comedy of Libanius is not. He is that much more practical.

7

All these *leges scholasticae* have received much discussion. On the one hand, the declaimer can of course be arbitrary; on the other, he has a wide field of law and legal theory to choose from, not only actual enactments but ideal or philosophical lawgiving. When Libanius makes Cephalus and Aristophon contend for a reward for 'a good life', he seems to be using a suggestion of the theorist Hippodamus, ideal rather than real.[95] When Hermogenes[96] uses the principle that a wrecked ship belongs to the man who stays on board, he may well be drawing on maritime law, perhaps that of Rhodes.[97] And when we hear of prosecution for failure to marry, we cannot say whether Plato's ideal city or the tradition of such legislation at Sparta is the source of the idea.

Or consider the cases in which, according to Diodorus,[98] three would-be legal reformers 'put their heads in the noose', as Charondas' code required, and proposed amendments in the law. One urged that if a one-eyed man were blinded, his attacker should lose both eyes. Another wanted it to be enacted that a woman who deserts her husband shall be forbidden to marry a younger man. Finally, a poor orphan begs that her kinsman shall marry her, and not have the option of a 500-drachma fine. True, we have no precise declamatory parallels to these themes; but they are clearly in the same line of thinking as many of the cases we do know. Sophistopolis has a theoretical or philosophical strain in its make-up. This perhaps makes it easier to understand its

[95] Liban. *Decl.* 15–16 (cf below, p. 120), Aristotle, *Pol.* 1268a.
[96] Hermogenes 85 Rabe.   [97] *Digest* 14.2 on *lex Rhodia de iactu*.
[98] Diodorus 12.17–18.

timelessness. Though set vaguely in the past — and written about in a language of the past — it has no precise time or place. The debt of the declaimers to classical oratory is, of course, enormous; but the society they assume has features absent from that of classical Athens. Nor is it precisely that of New Comedy, though this too is a genre to which they are much indebted. We must look also to other sources for affinities, literary or non-literary, with this strange but coherent world.

There are clearly links with the novel, but the novel itself, even if it originated in Hellenistic times, is too late to be in any sense the declaimers' inspiration. Nor is the reverse view — held in the past by Bornecque and Rohde[99] — that the declamation was the parent of the novel, likely to be true; though of course there are rhetorical and declamatory features in novels,[100] just as there are erotic and fanciful elements in declamation. Rather both are expressions of a common culture, which other kinds of literary fiction — comedy, mime and fable — also reflect. There are at any rate suggestive resemblances between all these forms and the declamation. For example the fable of 'The Old Woman and The Doctor'[101] is very like a declaimer's story: the doctor is treating an old lady for her bad eyesight and seizes the chance to steal

[99] Bornecque (1902) 89, 130; Rohde (1914) 339ff.
[100] 'Declamatory' features are naturally conspicuous in the trial scenes which are a common element in the novels: e.g. (i) Chariton 5.4–7, the case of Dionysius versus Mithridates before the King, in which (5.7) Mithridates shows that he might have entered a *paragraphē*, but declines to do so; (ii) Achilles Tatius 6.5ff, Clitophon accused of adultery; (iii) ibid. 7.7ff, his false confession to the murder of Leucippe, with Clinias' and Thersandros' speeches; (iv) ibid. 8.7ff, the case resumed, with Thersandros accusing the Priest of Artemis of interfering with the course of justice, and the Priest replying; note the advocates Sopatros and Nicostratus (both names of famous rhetors!), and esp. the way in which 'Sopatros' counters the accusation against Thersandros (a) by accusing the Priest of immorality, (b) by giving a laudatory account of Thersandros' youth and marriage; (v) Heliodorus 1.13ff, Cnemon's trial for an alleged attempt to murder his father (a false accusation engineered by his stepmother); the father's speech is rich in declamatory commonplaces, and the voting raises a problem also known in declamation (see above, n. 11). Occasionally, what is in effect a declamation is embedded in some other type of writing. Thus Maximus of Tyre, the 'philosophical' sophist, defends the contemplative life (*Or.* 16) by imagining Anaxagoras on trial before a court at Clazomenae for neglecting his property and playing no part in public affairs.
[101] B. E. Perry, *Babrius and Phaedrus* (Loeb edition), Appendix 57.

Sophistopolis, or the world of the Aristeus

her furniture; when she finds she cannot see it, she refuses to pay his fee. As to the mime, the powerful story in a papyrus mime[102] with its cruel adulteress and her victims, introduces many elements which recall the more sensational *meletai*. Again, riddles and jokes, ambivalent prophecies and unexpected turns of fortune, the stock-in-trade of any society in which verbal wit and pungent humour are highly valued, are at home in declamation also. Examples are easy to find. The prophet tries to ransom his daughter; the pirates say he can have her if he prophesies correctly whether he will get her or no; he says he will not; they are then caught in a trap, for if they give her back it will be contrary to their stipulation, and if they do not they will have failed to honour their obligation to return her if he forecasts the truth.[103] Or again: a man asks four prophets how he will die, and they give four different answers: what happens to him proves them all right – he is pursued by robbers, falls off a tree into a river, and is there devoured by a wild animal.[104]

This sort of culture, with its sharp, paradoxical and litigious wit, seems a perennial feature of the cities of the Aegean. It is perhaps worth citing a single tale, of no literary origin or pretension, from a much later date. E. D. Clarke, travelling in the Aegean in the early nineteenth century, reports from Cos what he takes to be a singular case of Turkish justice. A young man poisons himself for love of a girl, and her father is arrested, on the ground that if he had not had a daughter the young man would still be alive. He is fined 80 piastres for 'homicide by an intermediate cause'.[105] Turkish law, I am assured, is nothing like this. The tale is of the same genus as several in the declaimers: one thinks of the beautiful young man who never satisfied his lovers, but left town to avoid causing more suicides – and is accused of murder when he returns as a grown man.[106]

---

[102] *P. Oxy.* 413.
[103] *RG* IV.154. [104] *RG* IV.229.
[105] E. D. Clarke (1817) 449.
[106] *RG* IV.142. Cf also the case in Sopatros (*RG* VIII.182) in which a young man, imprisoned by his father because he loves a prostitute, breaks out of his prison and hangs himself when she visits him to reproach him with his subservience to his father; the father then charges her with responsibility for the young man's death.

3
Teachers and theories

> Scio plura inventuros adhuc qui legere antiquos studiosius volent, sed ne haec quoque excesserint modum vereor.
>
> 'I know that those who choose to read the ancients more carefully will find more; but I am afraid that even this has been too much.'
>
> Quintilian

I

The setting was, at least in theory, sugar for the pill of useful instruction. But what was the content and method of this instruction? It is easy to dismiss it as arid and pointless. After all, it is a commonplace that rhetoric does not make orators; does not Cicero go beyond the rules whenever his confidence in his own powers and judgement impels him to do so? But the teachers have much to tell us, and we cannot hope to appreciate *meletē* without entering into their characteristic theories.

Much of their argument was concerned with what they call *stasis* (Latin *status*).[1] Why the 'issue' should be called by this name was debated even in antiquity.[2] As with many technical terms, its metaphorical origins were forgotten. Was it the 'stance' of the orator, approaching his opponent like a wrestler at the beginning of a bout? Was it simply the 'quarrel', for *stasis* means 'dissension' or 'civil strife' in classical Greek? The term became fixed certainly by the time of Hermagoras, but the principle of distinguishing types of issue is of course much earlier: we saw it suggested by the plan of Antiphon's *Tetralogies*, while Quintilian[3] and others rightly saw the germs of it in Aristotle.

---

[1] See R. Nadeau, *GRBS* II (1952) 53–71; Barwick (1963) 52f. Handbooks of rhetoric (Martin [1974], Volkmann [1885]) contain general accounts of *stasis*-theory, as does Kennedy (1983) 73–86.

[2] Quint. 3.6.3. This chapter of Quintilian makes a good introduction to the subject: commentary in the separate ed. of Book 3 by J. Adamietz (1966).

[3] Ibid. 3.6.23ff.

Hermagoras, it seems, elaborated and codified previous thinking. The basic question – whether the issue was one of fact, definition or quality – had presented itself in much the same way to the teachers of the classical period. But it was Hermagoras, it seems, who made it a much more important part of the curriculum, and so is responsible for its dominant place in the teaching of the Roman period. True, we hear of a sophist at Athens in the third century A.D. who judged it all 'nonsense' and taught his pupils to say what they thought right on the spur of the moment without diagnosing the *stasis* at all. He was generally thought mad.[4] True also that there were many courses and treatises, clearly directed at *meletē* and using the typical themes as illustrations, which are not concerned with *stasis* or organized on this basis. Apsines of Gadara[5] offers an instance: his 'art' handles the 'parts' of a speech in order, and proceeds to illustrate types of speech in which particular treatment of individual parts is appropriate. In the prologue, for example, we praise audiences when they have previously taken good advice or achieved some success; this applies when we have Hermocrates urging the victorious Syracusans to sail against Athens. The point is that *meletē* is an advanced exercise, and presupposes not only this kind of instruction but the preliminary exercises of narrative, encomium and so on (*progymnasmata*), and, of course, grasp of stylistic propriety. But *stasis* remains the vital subject, and most of our knowledge of school declamation inevitably comes from the text-books that concentrate on it – notably Hermogenes and his commentators and Sopatros.

The number and arrangement of the *staseis* was, by the time of Hermogenes, a subject of warm and active controversy. On the one hand there was a commonly accepted scheme of thirteen distinct *staseis*, in which no distinction was made between genus and species. This was associated with Telephus of Pergamum[6]

[4] *RG* IV.38 (φλυαρία).
[5] Text in Sp.–H. 215ff. Apsines sees no need to discuss *staseis* (291.4) but gives detailed instruction on individual arguments which may be used.
[6] Telephus of Pergamum (*FGrHist* 505) was a celebrated rhetor and grammarian of the second century A.D., especially noted for his work on Homer, whom he regarded as the originator of rhetoric (*RG* V.7.23ff).

and Minucianus. The other, advocated by Hermogenes himself, attempted a more logical ordering of the material, proceeding largely by subdivision. This shows an increasing concern for theoretical elegance; and some time in the third century, a school of teachers arose – we know the names of Evagoras and Aquila – who sought to introduce even more philosophical rigour into the system.[7] In this they were followed by professed philosophers, notably the great Neoplatonists Porphyrius and Syrianus. There had indeed been earlier scholars who had been proficient in both rhetoric and philosophy – Plutarch comes to mind, and Philostratus recalls Herodes and Aristocles[8] – but the existence of really distinguished professionals equally at home in both disciplines is a phenomenon of this later period, from the fourth to the sixth century. This philosophical intervention may be judged unhelpful. The commentators on Hermogenes, among whom Syrianus was particularly influential, seem much more concerned with the arrangement of their own material than with any utility which the system might offer either for the potential speaker or for the reader of Demosthenes.[9] Syrianus and Sopatros are forever explaining not only what Hermogenes meant but why he put things in a particular order.[10] In Sopatros' *Diaireseis*, which is more practical in scope, the order followed is a modification of Hermogenes', with features due to Minucianus.[11] Doubtless, there were almost as many schemes as there were schools.

[7] Evagoras and Aquila: *RG* IV.583, Kennedy (1983) 79.
[8] See Philostratus, *VS* 571.
[9] Rhetorical comment on Demosthenes and the other Attic orators, involving analysis of the issue (i.e. *stasis*) goes back to Hellenistic times: Lossau (1964) 111ff. But the vagaries are apparent, and the truth is that most classical speeches admit of different interpretations from this point of view. Thus Lycurgus' 'Against Leocrates' is an accusation of treason, in which the defendant alleged (i) that his departure from Athens did not count as treason, (ii) that his intention was not treasonable, but (iii) was commercial. The ancient argument to the speech gives three diagnoses of the *stasis* as alternatives propounded by rival rhetors: (i) *horos antonomazōn* (cf below, n. 38); (ii) *stochasmos apo gnōmēs* ('conjecture from intention'); (iii) *antistasis*. All may be said to be right.
[10] See esp. *RG* IV.767, where 'later and more philosophic' theorists are said to put *metalēpsis* after *antithesis* because it 'resolves' *dikaiologia*; it should at any rate precede the 'legal issues'. All this is arguing not about the subject but about the best order of lessons in the text-book.
[11] Cf above, ch. 1, n. 24.

2

The first question which any speaker has to confront is whether there is really a case for a judge to decide. Hermagoras put this by asking whether the question (*zētēma*) is 'consistent' (*synestēke*, συνέστηκε) – we might say 'hangs together'. Problems that do not meet this requirement were generally called *asystata*, and the later rhetors, following Hermagoras' lead, tried to identify various types. If a teacher proposed such a theme to his pupils, he was guilty of the same sort of mistake as the modern mathematical examiner who sets an insoluble problem. Hermogenes[12] gives a list of eight kinds of 'non-problems', and several others which he thinks are nearly as bad; his motive is no doubt to criticize his rivals as much as to help his students. The list is as follows.

(i) The 'one-sided' (*monomeres*), in which the arguments on one side are overwhelming: e.g. a brothel-keeper digs a pit and catches in it ten young men who have finished dinner and are proceeding towards his establishment in a drunken party; he kills them, and is accused of murder.

(ii) 'The totally equal' (*isazon diolou*): e.g. two rich young men have pretty wives; each detects the other coming out of the wrong house, and they mutually accuse each other of adultery.

(iii) 'The convertible' (*kata to antistrephon*): e.g. a creditor demands both loan and interest, but the debtor alleges the money was a deposit, not a loan, so that no interest is owing; while the case is pending, the *dēmos* enacts a cancellation of debts,[13] whereupon they both change their ground, the creditor now claiming the money back as a deposit, and the debtor saying that it was indeed a debt and has therefore been cancelled. The proofs they adduce are neither distinct from each other nor strong; they both fall victim to their own arguments.[14]

(iv) 'The insoluble' (*aporon*). In these cases, no end or solution

---

[12] 32ff Rabe. I paraphrase and abridge.
[13] 'Cancellation of debts' (χρεῶν ἀποκοπαί) was an extreme measure thought characteristic of revolution within the city state: see Plutarch, *Solon* 15, Pl. *Rep.* 566A, *Laws* 736C.
[14] περιπετεῖς τοῖς ἑαυτῶν ἄμφω γίνονται λόγοις.

can be found. 'Alexander dreams that he is not to believe in dreams; he takes counsel. Whatever advice is given him in these circumstances, it will result in the opposite.'

(v) 'The implausible' (*apithanon*): e.g. if one imagines Socrates keeping a brothel or Aristides committing an injustice.

(vi) 'The impossible' (*adynaton*): e.g. if one supposes the Siphnians or Maronites to be debating empire over the Greeks, or the oracle of Delphi telling a lie.[15]

(vii) 'The disreputable' (*adoxon*): e.g. a man hires out his wife and then goes to law to recover the fee from the person who hired her. There seems no reason why this should not be a subject of dispute, and indeed Roman law seems to envisage the possibility of a husband's profiting from his wife's infidelity. But this is not the view of the Greek commentators: Syrianus[16] judges that the case is so monstrous that the jury will have made up its mind before the proceedings begin; Marcellinus thinks it is too horrible to occur in real life.

(viii) 'The uncircumstantial' (*aperistaton*): e.g. 'a man disowns his son for no reason'. No argument can be produced about a purely arbitrary act.

3
Stochasmos (*coniectura*)

All our authors begin with 'conjecture', the type of case in which the sole issue is one of fact. Seneca indeed makes it clear that a 'division' of such cases is not expected;[17] and 'conjectures' play a very small part in his collection of themes. So it may well be that the elaborate *diaireseis* or 'divisions' we find in Hermogenes and his successors are in fact a later development; the more so

---

[15] This naturally caused the commentators difficulty. The case of the insignificant cities of Siphnos and Maroneia is really 'implausible' rather than 'impossible', but Hermogenes seems to have wished to separate the morally inappropriate cases of category (v) from these. The Delphi example presumably rests on the idea that it is of the essence of the god's nature to tell the truth, and so he *cannot* lie.

[16] *RG* IV.162–4. Sopatros rightly draws attention to the influence of Aeschines' *Against Timarchus* on this theme.

[17] *Contr.* 7.3.6; Fairweather (1981) 159. Hermogenes' account is at 43ff Rabe.

since they involve elements which belong primarily to other *staseis*, and make the defendant do more than simply prove a fact. In Hermogenes there are no less than ten 'headings'. These are, it is important to note, headings of argument, not parts of the speech. Hermogenes does not, as does Sopatros, give explicit instructions for *prooimia*, *katastasis* or epilogue; all this is presumably taken for granted in his exposition, which seeks to expose the logical structure of the case rather than the literary economy of the speech.

(i) The 'division' begins with a topic which has nothing to do with proving whether the alleged fact happened or not. This is the 'demurrer' (*paragraphikon*), the claim that there is no ground for action or that it is being brought in the wrong court or at the wrong time. Where this is the main issue, we have the separate *stasis* of *metalēpsis*;[18] here it is mentioned as a good move to make if it can be made. If successful, of course, it makes everything else pointless. If the ten young bachelors accused of evil living can persuade the court that their cases should be taken separately, the case against them as a group collapses. If the cowardly husband who accuses his wife of adultery because her son has turned out a brave man cannot show why he failed to proceed against her at the time of the alleged offence, his accusation carries no weight.

(ii) The second element in Hermogenes' *diairesis*, on the other hand, is clearly germane to an inquiry into fact, and not to anything else. It is the 'demand for proofs' (*elenchōn apaitēsis*). You are to put awkward questions to your opponent, asking for whatever kind of testimony he finds most difficult to provide. Sopatros explains:

If there are no witnesses, say that the presence of witnesses is the strongest demonstration; if there are, discredit them. If the evidence consists of facts, ask for witnesses, and make light of probable conclusions; if there *are* witnesses, set a high value on probability.[19]

A declamation of Libanius[20] gives an exact illustration. A

---

[18] Below, §6.   [19] *RG* VIII.7.18.
[20] *Decl.* 44; the quotation is from §17.

foreigner illegally attends an assembly, and claims to have important secret information for the government. The general however not only forbids him to speak but has him put to death. There follows a *coup d'état*, and an attempt is made to establish a tyranny. This is frustrated, but the general who had ordered the foreigner's death is accused of having been privy to the plot. The defence has an easy line to take:

You say I was involved in the conspiracy and had a part in the attempt to establish tyranny? Good. Let anyone who knows this come forward and give evidence, show himself to the judges, persuade them (sworn as they are) that if they kill me they will not be false to their jurors' oath. That is what a real accusation is. 'The man has stolen': what proof is there? X bears witness. 'The defendant has committed adultery.' How can we be sure? From the evidence... Summon the witnesses to your accusation, be they free men or slaves, archers, infantrymen, cavalry, slingers, citizens or foreigners. The difference between democracy and tyranny is that, in a tyranny, it is enough for the master to give the order, and the man must die, whereas here an accused person cannot be sentenced to death until he has been proved to have committed a crime deserving that punishment.

This is a skilful move. The 'demand for proof' is plainly put, and at the same time the general displays his love of the democratic system: how could such a man be privy to such a conspiracy?

(iii) and (iv) Next come the twin topics of 'will' and 'ability' (*boulēsis* and *dynamis*[21]). Did the defendant have the desire to do what he is alleged to have done? Did he also have the ability? These arguments are based not on evidence, but on probability: they follow, as Hermogenes points out from the personal characteristics of the persons concerned. The 'topics of encomium'[22] are therefore relevant: family, upbringing, education, physical and moral qualities, pursuits, action, opportunities – all this gives material from which the themes of 'will' and

---

[21] Sopatros often gives headings in the dative, and here has βουλήσει καὶ δυνάμει. We understand, e.g., χρήσῃ 'you will use'. The principle of 'will and means' was used in early rhetoric, e.g. in Gorgias' *Palamedes*.

[22] Good account in Burgess (1902) 118–27.

'ability' can be developed. Sopatros explains their use in the case of 'Alcibiades accused of aiming at tyranny':

For the defence, the aim of the topic of 'will' is to demolish the reasons for which it might have been plausible for him to choose to be tyrant; for the prosecution, it is to establish these same reasons. Some say that the topic of 'ability' is missing in this case, because it is admitted (by both sides) that Alcibiades had the ability to be tyrant; my view, however, is that, even if he *could* have done it, this ability is removed by his lack of will...It is impossible to do something unless you want to, and useless to want unless the action is possible.[23]

This reasoning is valid only if 'ability' is held to include the possession of a character which makes the action possible; in other words, a determination that can be exercised in the individual act of 'willing'.

(v) There follows a section clumsily headed 'from beginning to end';[24] this is a sort of narrative, usually on the prosecutor's part, in which the course of events is seen as a series of natural consequences, and inferences are drawn from what happened to the defendant's guilt. Hermogenes gives an example which his commentators discuss at length.[25] A man suspects a slave of a guilty relationship with his wife, locks him up, and himself goes abroad. But it is the practice to release prisoners at the Thesmophoria, and the wife, in her husband's absence, takes advantage of this to free the slave. The master of the house is found dead, apparently on his way home. The body has not been robbed. The slave has disappeared. The wife is accused of complicity in murder. This is a 'complex' *stochasmos*, as more than one fact is in dispute; and the topic 'from beginning to end' begins with the husband's suspicion and goes as far as the wife's alleged complicity in the murder. The prosecutor shows how all this hangs together.

Hermogenes also[26] cites a case in which both sides use the

---

[23] *RG* VIII.10.5ff. Cf below, ch. 6, pp. 123ff.
[24] ἀπ' ἀρχῆς ἄχρι τέλους. Volkmann ([1885] 377 n. 1) suggested that the phrase was taken from Demosthenes' *De corona* 177 (ἀπὸ τῆς ἀρχῆς διὰ πάντων ἄχρι τῆς τελευτῆς διεξῆλθον).
[25] Hermogenes 58 Rabe; *RG* IV.355, V.145, VIII.67ff (Sopatros).
[26] 47 Rabe.

topic. A man whose brother is accused of aiming at tyranny distinguishes himself in battle. He is therefore allowed to choose his reward; and he requests that the charge against his brother should be dropped. The brother of course does become tyrant; the hero kills him, and is then himself accused of complicity in the original plot. Here the prosecution expounds 'from beginning to end' the circumstances in which the case against the brother was dropped, while the defendant dwells on the events leading up to his act of tyrannicide.

(vi) and (vii) The terms *antilēpsis* and *metalēpsis* in this context, mean something like 'plea' and 'counterplea'; Syrianus[27] conjectures that *antilēpsis* is a metaphor taken from the plight of a man swept downstream by his accuser's attack but clutching at a rock or a tree that blocks the current; if *stasis* were originally the wrestler's stance, the 'grip' would be his hold on the opponent, and this is perhaps a more likely explanation. *Metalēpsis* is the other side's response to this. The boy who 'beautifies himself' and is accused of being a prostitute[28] may 'clutch at the plea' that there is nothing forbidden about his choice of clothes or jewelry or cosmetics; and his accuser can either sweep this right away by a flat denial ('counterplea by objection', *metalēpsis kat' enstasin*) or say that the actions complained of may be permissible in general but are forbidden in the particular circumstances of the case: this is called *metalēpsis kat' antiparastasin*, 'counterplea by rejoinder'.

(viii) Next in Hermogenes' list comes *metathesis aitias* 'shift of cause'. This is a plea by the defendant that the intention of his actions or words should be taken into account. Examples are common. A rich man has called out to the prisoners in the gaol that they will soon be free; he asks that this should be taken as a word spoken late at night, as a drunken jest, not as evidence that he wants to be tyrant. Similarly, the rich youth gazing at the acropolis in tears explains his emotion not as envy but as sympathy for people living under the heel of a tyrant. Or again, the murder suspect who has been found burying the body explains that he was passing by, and it is a pious duty to bury

[27] RG IV.369. [28] Hermogenes 48.18 Rabe.

the dead. This type of argument is also called *chrōma*, in Latin *color*; a term familiar from Seneca.[29]

Antilēpsis (vi) and *metathesis* (viii) naturally go together and form the defendant's answer to 'from beginning to end' (v). So in Sopatros' defence of Alcibiades:

> You should refute [the prosecution's account of events 'from beginning to end'] by *antilēpsis* and *chrōma*. *Antilēpsis*: 'it was open to me to accept what gift I asked [he has asked for a bodyguard as reward for his victory at Cyzicus], for no law objects...' You can expand the *antilēpsis* by reading the law and examining it in detail. *Chrōma*: 'I chose this reward because I am envied and have many enemies.' You can then substantiate the *chrōma* from past events: 'When there were such attacks and such malice directed against me before I had had any success like the present victory at Cyzicus – when those who were sick with jealousy against me were eager for my death – how could their zeal fail to be even greater now?'[30]

(ix) *Pithanē apologia* – 'persuasive defence' – is a somewhat obscure name for a particular form of defence argument, in which the accused uses some fact which the prosecution had brought against him and gives it an interpretation in his own interest. The man found in tears at the foot of the acropolis can now say: 'If I had wanted to be tyrant, I should not have disclosed my feelings by weeping in public; the very fact on which you base the charge actually proves my innocence!' This move of course is not always possible. If the evidence for an attempt at tyranny is the secret hoarding of arms, we cannot make the accused argue that he would not have stored the weapons if he had wanted to be tyrant. In this case, the best thing would be to urge that the possession of arms does not necessarily entail the intention to subvert the constitution. Sopatros' Alcibiades, with his bodyguard, does however have a 'persuasive defence':

> If I had wanted to be tyrant, I should not have asked for this reward... The murderer does not walk around with a bloody sword, the poisoner does not display his destructive material in public... How

---

[29] *chrōma*: *RG* VIII.49 (definition), VIII.13, IV.397, VII.308 etc.; Volkmann (1885) 113, Fairweather (1981) 166.

[30] *RG* VIII.13.5ff; below, ch. 6, p. 128.

then could I, if I had wanted to be tyrant, have asked for this gift, making myself so obvious?[31]

(x) Finally, some advice on the epilogue; Hermogenes puts this under the head *koinē poiotēs*, 'common quality'. A prosecutor must attack the offence, expose the defendant's lies, and so on; the defendant must sum up and try to excite pity. This is the time for him to produce a wife or children or friends. The prosecutor derides all this. Both parties make use of what are called 'heads of purpose' (*telika kephalaia*) – i.e. the notions of legality, justice, expediency, possibility and reputation.[32] All this is common doctrine, valid in any case, not only in *stochasmoi*.

The various types of *stochasmos* and the order in which they should be taught were also much discussed. It was a problem, for example, whether there could be a case with no known facts: a man disappears, his dissolute son is charged with murder.[33] Complex cases, in which more than one issue of fact is involved, are naturally common. The rhetors distinguished two classes: one in which one issue was 'incidental' to the other, one in which one issue was 'prior' to the other. The distinction is not difficult to see. A rich man swears to become tyrant,[34] and a poor man swears to kill a tyrant. The poor man is found dead. The rich man is then accused of attempting tyranny. Here the question at issue is that of the attempt at tyranny. But 'incidental' to it (*empiptōn*) is the question whether the rich man murdered the poor man. Compare this with the text-book instance of 'prior conjecture' (*prokataskeuazomenos*),[35] in which a rich general kills the three sons of a poor man as traitors, two after failing to extort confessions by torture, the third when he does confess. Their father does not prosecute, and is therefore accused of complicity in their plot to betray the city to the enemy. The question at issue

[31] *RG* VIII.13.20ff.

[32] Lists of headings of this sort naturally occur in all rhetorical teaching: Aristotle, *Rhet.* 1.3, *Rhet. ad Alex.* 1.3ff (pp. 17ff Fuhrmann), Cic. *Inv.* 2.156, Aphthonius, *Progymn.* 17.14 Rabe, etc. The lists vary; Volkmann (1885) 300ff gives details of some variants. See also below, §7.

[33] *RG* IV.431ff.

[34] *RG* VIII.51.

[35] Hermogenes 57 Rabe, Sopatros, *RG* VIII.32.

is the father's guilt. But prior to it is the question of the guilt of the first two sons. If this is not established, the conspiracy charge will hardly stand.

Some of the best theoretical discussion relates to these cases. Hermogenes[36] gives the following as an example of 'incidental conjecture'. A general has been convicted of treason, and is imprisoned by his colleague – apparently in the colleague's house – until he names his accomplices. He never does so, for he is shortly put to death by the colleague who alleges he has found him 'with his wife'. The colleague is then accused of complicity in the original treason. This *plasma* was greatly admired.[37] Its ingenuity lay in the imprisonment of the suspect in the house, and in the idea that it was likely for a conspirator to want to get rid of someone who might turn evidence against him. The 'incidental' question – which is whether the imprisoned general did in fact seduce his colleague's wife – arises naturally out of the *chrōma*, that is to say the accused's reason for the killing, which would otherwise be strong evidence for his involvement in the plot. Now if the adultery had been certain, the killing would have been justified, and the case would not have been brought in this form. As it was only suspected, the probability of it has to be argued: could a prisoner have done it, and would the wife have lent herself to it? And this whole discussion of the 'incidental' question comes somewhere in the course of the main discussion – at any rate before the accused makes his 'persuasive defence', and tries to show that it does not follow from his having killed the man that he had been his fellow-conspirator. The result could be a highly ingenious and complex speech.

4
Horos (*finitio*)

If the facts are admitted, the definition of them may still be in doubt. A man has stolen private property out of a temple: is his offence robbery or sacrilege? If the former, he restores, it may be, double the amount; if the latter, he dies. This was the type

[36] 50 Rabe.
[37] *RG* IV.453ff (Marcellinus); VIII.52.11 (Sopatros); Apsines 267 Sp.–H.

example from earliest times; discussed by Aristotle, it is still being worked by Sopatros and his pupils.[38] But more complex cases are commoner. A son is disowned for living with a hetaira. He dies, and she buries him in her family tomb. The father removes the body to bury with his own people. Is this tomb-robbery or not?[39] Again: who deserves the tyrannicide's reward, when the man who went to kill the tyrant only scared him away, and it was someone who met him accidentally who actually did the deed?[40]

As with *stochasmos*, there are elaborate *diaireseis*. Hermogenes again has ten sections.[41]

The first is (i) *probolē*, the 'presentation' of the case. If there is a preliminary narrative, this follows immediately, and it is essentially a statement of the facts. The rhetor who has persuaded a tyrant to abdicate and claims a tyrannicide's reward explains that it was he who suppressed the tyranny. His opponent then offers (ii) the strict *horos*, that tyrannicide involves killing. The retort (iii) is called *anthorismos*, counter-definition, and asserts that to suppress a tyrant is enough to meet the conditions. This is expanded (iv) in the *syllogismos*, 'inference', where it is shown that the consequences are the same. But (v) what did the lawgiver really intend (*gnōmē nomothetou*)? Anyway (vi), it is an important matter ('importance', *pēlikotēs*) and peaceful suppression is actually preferable to violence (vii, 'relative importance', *pros ti*). In the case before us, a counter-charge (viii, *antithesis*) is impossible; but if, for example, we were defending the husband accused of murder because the man he has killed as his wife's lover turns out to be a eunuch,[42] then it would be open to us to say that the man deserved to die, even if he only did what he could;

[38] Aristotle, *Rhet.* I.13.1374a2, Quint. 2.6.41, Hermogenes 37 Rabe, Sopatros in *RG* VIII.102. This case was an example of *horos antonomazōn*, 'counter-naming definition'.

[39] Sopatros in *RG* VIII.78.

[40] *RG* VIII.98. [41] Hermogenes 59ff Rabe.

[42] We recall the case of the sophist Favorinus, the great rival of Polemon, whose life was paradoxical in three ways: he spoke Greek though he was a Gaul (he came from Arles), he was tried for adultery though he was a eunuch, he quarrelled with the emperor and survived (Philostratus, *VS* 489). Fiction and life once again coincide. Is Favorinus' case the rhetors' source?

and this in turn could be countered by the argument that he should have been charged with the offence and not summarily put to death. The conclusion of a *horos*-speech, as in *stochasmos*, is based (ix) on 'quality' (*poiotēs*), the character of the defendant, and (x) on 'intention' (*gnōmē*), the purpose of the action or the prosecution.

There were also, inevitably, arguments about the classes of definition. There were 'double' and 'incidental' definitions, and various types of dispute concerning rewards. The rhetors are by no means in agreement about the classification;[43] the importance of 'reward' cases in school practice doubtless encouraged a good deal of refinement of this sort, as many of these are of necessity cases of definition.[44]

A single example may suffice to illustrate the application of the *diairesis*.[45] Both Hermogenes and Sopatros cite as *empiptōn horos*, 'incidental definition', what we may call 'the case of the Mysteries'. A man dreams that the secrets of Eleusis are revealed to him. On waking, he describes what he has seen to an initiate, and asks if it corresponds to the truth. The initiate does not answer in words, but nods assent. Is he then guilty of having revealed the sacred truths? Two 'definitions' are involved here. The primary one is whether 'nodding' constitutes revealing. 'Incidental' to this is the question whether the dream amounts to an initiation. Sopatros discusses this in great detail. He begins with one or two general points. Both contenders are pious people, and

[43] Thus Hermogenes has, in addition to 'simple' definition, five more complex kinds: *antonomazōn* (above, n. 38), *kata syllēpsin* ('by comprehension', in which it is to be shown that the act is a species of a genus falling under the definition in question), *kata prosōpa* ('by persons'), *empiptōn* ('incidental') and *dyo horoi* ('two definitions'). Sopatros' classification is different: *kata krisin* ('in judgement'), *kat' axiōsin* ('in expectation', e.g. the case of the lover claiming exemption from service as 'sick'), *kat' aitēsin* ('in demand', e.g. does the rhetor deserve the tyrannicide's reward that he demands for having persuaded the man to abdicate?); *kat' amphisbētēsin* ('in dispute', again with reference to reward cases), as well as some of Hermogenes' classes. This kind of confusion, in which logical classification gives ground before pedagogic need, is characteristic of Sopatros' less rigorous but in some ways more practical approach.

[44] Cf *RG* VIII.393, where 'reward' cases are said to be either 'definitions' or 'pragmatic'.

[45] *RG* VIII.110–124 (Sopatros), Hermogenes 64 Rabe.

this must be brought out. As to organization, the case proceeds as a simple *horos* 'as far as relative importance' – i.e. (vii) in Hermogenes' scheme – and the 'incidental' *horos* then takes over. 'Definition' is by nature dry (*xēros*), and a great deal of illustration is needed to make it interesting. Six *prooimia* and an elaborate narrative or *katastasis* display Sopatros' facility; there is ample scope here for traditional encomia of Athens and of the Mysteries. But there are also dangers: the defendant must beware lest, in expatiating on his own religious feelings, or in telling the story of the dream, he inadvertently reveals some point of mystic doctrine, and so exposes himself to the very charge against which he is making his defence. All this is set out at great length, with elaborate *ēthopoiia* and other devices for prolonging and amplifying the narrative. The argumentation itself begins with the *probolē*: the prosecutor is made to say 'you broke the law by nodding'. The answer to this (*anthorismos*) is that 'nodding' is not the same as 'telling'. This needs amplification in the *syllogismos*, (iv): nodding is as different from telling as shipbuilding from steering or making torches from carrying a torch in the mystic procession. And what was the 'lawgiver's intention' (v)? The law says 'tell' without any addition or qualification. Of course it is an important matter (*pēlikotēs* [vi]); conventional remarks (*thesis*) on the value of silence will serve to establish this. 'Relative importance' (vii) in this context means showing that piety towards the gods is more important than any other virtue, and that the 'nod', which could reveal nothing to the uninitiated, was a demonstration of a truly pious attitude.

This naturally introduces the 'incidental' definition. The prosecution alleged that the defendant revealed secrets to an uninitiated person. This is not so; and the proof of it is conducted by the same stages as any other *horos* ([iv] to [vii] in Hermogenes' list). Thus *syllogismos* (iv) shows that the dreamer is indeed an initiate, instructed by the goddesses themselves and not by the hierophants. 'Lawgiver's intention' (v) has strictly no relevance; but it is easily replaced by the goddesses' intentions, which must have been to demonstrate by the dream that they established the Mysteries, and can initiate whom they will. 'Importance' (vi) is obvious: it is a great and wonderful thing to be initiated in this way. Indeed (vii), one might perhaps say that it is a greater privilege than to be initiated in the ordinary manner. Gods cannot make mistakes; their human agents can. One would think this an obvious move; it is thus interesting that Sopatros puts it cautiously:[46] '"Relative importance" is lacking' in this case, 'unless you choose to compare the initiation in the dream with those initiated by the hierophant'. The rhetorical danger will be that of giving offence to the establishment; behind this perhaps lies the feeling that direct revelations are somewhat suspect. The speech now moves forward towards its end; there had apparently been something of an epilogue already, at the point where the main definition was abandoned for the incidental one, but the chief place for display of piety and encouragement is clearly at the end of the whole speech:

Now is the time, members of the jury, to lead this man to the secret rites of Eleusis and teach him what he has learned in riddles from the goddesses.

Indeed, the visionary (whom the speaker now addresses directly) will have something to tell us:

Teach us if we are in any way wrong; add what is missing to our practices. You may well know more than we, since Kore and Demeter themselves have initiated you.

5
Poiotēs (qualitas)

If there is no question of fact, and no doubt that the action in dispute satisfies the proposed definition, there may still be an issue to be debated. The action may be just or unjust, legal or illegal, expedient or inexpedient. This is what Hermagoras called 'by accident' (*kata symbebēkos*) because the question depends on 'accidents' of the matter under debate. In Cicero it appears as *controversia de genere* or *generalis*; but its commonest name is *poiotēs*, 'quality'.

If we follow Hermogenes,[47] this category of issue divides first

[46] *RG* VIII.123.6.   [47] 37ff Rabe.

into questions about written law and questions about actions. Of these, the first type is set aside to be dealt with later; these are *staseis nomikai*. The second type (*staseis logikai*) again divides, this time into questions relating to the future and questions relating to the past. Now questions concerning the future are traditionally the area of deliberative oratory, not of forensic. These 'pragmatic' issues (*pragmatikai*) may therefore again be discarded from the main scheme; Hermogenes in fact treats them separately and so do most of our teachers. There remains the category of issues of right and expediency relating to the past (*dikaiologia*). This forms the main subject of study. Once again, there is a division into two. The defendant may either claim outright that what he did was justified, or admit that it was wrong but offer an excuse or a counter-charge to show that it was not really his fault. The first of these types of claim, which the Latin rhetors sensibly called *constitutio iuridicialis absoluta*, passes in Greek under the name *antilēpsis*. The second (in Latin not *absoluta* but *adsumptiva*) is called *antithesis*. That these terms have other uses, not always closely analogous, is just unfortunate.

As type examples of *antilēpsis*, Hermogenes and Sopatros use rather similar cases. In Hermogenes, a painter is accused of an offence against the state[48] because he has set up a picture of a shipwreck in a place where sailors see it as they approach the city's harbour, to the great detriment of trade. In Sopatros,[49] it is the painter Mikon who is charged because he has made the Persians bigger than the Greeks in a picture of the battle of Marathon.

---

[48] 65ff Rabe. Bonner (1949) 98, points out that 'doing wrong to the *dēmos*' was a punishable offence at Athens, but he doubts whether there was any special form of indictment. Xen. *Hell.* 1.7.20, which he quotes, itself gives ample ground for the rhetors' use of the concept of δημόσιον ἀδίκημα: the 'psephism of Kannonos', we are there told, 'ordains that if anyone wrongs the Athenian people, he shall defend his case in bonds in the assembly'. We observe that Hermogenes assumes that only persons with public responsibilities can be so charged, though Syrianus' commentary (*RG* IV.595) adduces cases of private citizens.

[49] *RG* VIII.126ff. Mikon, son of Phanomathos, was the artist of various paintings in the Theseion and Stoa Poikile, and also a sculptor: Lippold, *RE* XV.1557ff.

Teachers and theories

Hermogenes' division — it is only an indication of the headings, not a full *diairesis* — has fifteen heads. This is a more complex *stasis* than the first two. First (i) comes the presentation of the charge (*probolē*), which in effect means a short statement of the facts and their implications. The next two items, (ii) 'part of justice' (*morion dikaiou*) and (iii) 'person' (*prosōpon*) amount to a double objection to the case: the defendant argues, first, that he should not be prosecuted for something which no law forbids, and secondly that private citizens cannot be charged with 'offences against the state', since they have no responsibility for public affairs, and only politicians (*rhētores*) and generals are liable. Sopatros (after his five or six *prooimia* and a grandiose *katastasis* on the battle of Marathon) has the second of these points only; he says it is obligatory in such cases, when a private citizen is accused of a 'public' offence.[50] After this — to judge from Sopatros, this could be a very considerable part of the speech both for defence and for prosecution — the defence turns (iv) to definition (*horos*), urging that painting a picture is not the sort of thing covered by the charge of 'public offences', which really applies to acts like the betrayal of ships, forts or allies.[51] From this point, both sides proceed on the lines laid down for *horos*: counter-definition, inference, lawgiver's intention, importance and relative importance (v–ix). What follows (x–xi) is again already familiar: *antilēpsis* and *metalēpsis*, the defendant alleging (with arguments this time) that painting is a perfectly legitimate activity, and the prosecution contesting this by saying that this does not apply on this occasion, because the practice of the art is indeed permitted, but not its use to cause damage or distress.[52] Both Hermogenes and Sopatros follow this (xii) with a so-called 'antistatic' objection or *chrōma* in which the defendant claims to have painted the picture for good reasons — to help sailors or (in Mikon's case) to magnify the achievement of the victorious Greeks. This can be answered sarcastically (*eirōneia*) or by a further *metalēpsis* (xiii)

[50] *RG* VIII.132.1; 135.16. Cf above n. 48; Sopatros here follows a tradition distinct from that of Hermogenes.
[51] I.e. characteristic acts of treason; cf. Hyperides *For Euxenippus* 22 (Bonner, loc. cit.). [52] Cf *RG* VIII.139.7.

suggesting that, if he wanted to help, the painter should have done it in some more acceptable way. But (xiv), 'we all do what we can, according to our several capacities'. Sopatros' Mikon[53] advances a further argument, not in Hermogenes' sketch: the picture can be erased. This is answered by saying that its evil effects, the lack of confidence it engendered, will not disappear so easily; and anyway the proposal is itself an admission of wrong. Sopatros adds an interesting parallel: Polemon, he tells us, did not use this argument in his treatment of the case brought against Alcibiades for having a representation of the Sicilian disaster engraved on his drinking cups, because the memory of Sicily would have endured even if the offending cups had been melted down.[54] We know of a similar theme about Thucydides, who offers to burn his history[55] – only to be answered by the objection that people who have got copies will not destroy them.

The term 'antistatic' objection, which we saw in this last *diairesis*, is also part of a set of terms which provides the subdivisions of the second main class of *dikaiologia*, the type called in Latin *adsumptiva*, and in Greek *antithetikē*. These defences admit error but excuse it or turn the blame elsewhere. Speeches in which such a defence is essential are grouped under four heads though these are rather variously arranged in the different authors.[56] In *antistasis* (i), the main argument is that the action avoided worse consequences; the type case is that of the general who used tombstones to build a wall and is accused of impiety.[57] *Metastasis* (ii) transfers the blame to some unavoidable circumstance: the general who has thrown the dead overboard in a storm pleads overwhelming necessity. (iii) In the third type (*antenklēma*,

[53] Ibid. 142.3ff.

[54] Cf Hermogenes 68 Rabe. Sopatros seems to be our only evidence for Polemon's use of this theme, which is however mentioned (though not attached to Alcibiades' name) by Hermogenes' commentators (see *RG* IV.233, 608; V.94, 96, 318; VI.621).

[55] *RG* IV.619 (Syrianus). Thucydides was often regarded as having been unfair to his own country (*Vita* 2.4, p. 201 Westermann).

[56] Sopatros' order is apparently that of Minucianus (*RG* V.173: cf above, ch. 1, n. 24).

[57] [Liban.] *Decl.* 34 is a parody of this sort of argument: a miserly father disowns his son because he has vowed a talent to Asclepius for the father's recovery. The son says (this is the *antistasis*) that it was all for the father's good.

'counter-charge') the victim is shown to have deserved what was coming to him. An example[58] is the husband who makes assignations with his own wife, accuses her of adultery, dismisses her, and keeps the dowry. He goes through this procedure twice, with two sisters, and it is only when he is with the third sister that the trusting father of all three girls catches up with him, and he comes to be accused of murder. The plea is that the husband's crimes deserve death. Finally, (iv) the defendant may ask forgiveness (*syngnōmē*). A father tells one son to kill another, but instead the young man warns his brother and sends him out of the country for his safety. He is therefore disowned by the father. His plea is that he took pity on his brother. The response is that it was pity for the wrong person – it was the father who deserved it.[59]

The *diairesis* of such cases includes few elements which we have not already encountered.[60] Sopatros' handling of one type case – the general who used tombstones to strengthen the wall – may be sufficient to show the principle.[61] After the *katastasis*, we would normally expect (i) a 'demurrer by definition' (*horos paragraphikos*), but this is hardly possible in this case, since the misuse of the tombs is undoubtedly impiety. So (ii) the charge is stated at once, with the whole circumstances ('from beginning to end', *ap' archēs achri telous*). It is answered (iii) by an *antistasis* – 'I did it for your sake, and we won'. Intention (*dianoia*) is an important point in this sort of case, and the general now argues (iv) that the charge against him could only have been justified if he could be shown to have had a sinister aim in view. But this is certainly not the case. He was acting within his powers (v, an *antilēpsis*), and he did it for the sake of the city's freedom (vi). Both sides in such cases are recommended to use the trick called *biaios horos*, 'violent definition', in which the speaker throws his opponent's interpretation back in his face.[62] In this case, (vii) the defendant could say that his use of the tombstones 'for necessary

---

[58] Liban. *Decl.* 40, *RG* VIII.229, Minucianus 350 Sp.–H. Cf above, p. 34.
[59] *RG* VIII.244ff.
[60] Hermogenes' *diairesis* (72ff Rabe) is of the case in which an *aristeus* has killed his prostitute son, and differs somewhat from Sopatros.
[61] *RG* VIII.198ff.   [62] On this see now Pernot (1981) 70.

purposes'[63] is no impiety at all, because it means that we make the dead fight on our side and help to defend their country. The *metalēpsis* 'you ought to have fortified the city in some other way' is naturally available to the prosecution (viii), and is answered (ix) by a plea of necessity and haste (*metastasis*). Epilogues (x) follow the usual pattern, with emphasis on the characteristics and intentions of the parties involved.

There are many such cases; 'antitheticals' were a popular exercise.

6
Metalēpsis (*translatio*)

We have seen more than once that it is a common opening move to allege that the case should not be tried, either because the court is not competent or for some other reason – for example, that it is an unreasonably long time after the event. This is to 'enter a demurrer' (*paragraphesthai*). If it succeeds, the defence needs no other argument. This plea is clearly often advanced when there can hardly be more than a distant hope of its succeeding, and the speaker has other arguments ready and proceeds to them without much delay. But there are cases in which a *metalēpsis* is likely to succeed; these constitute a separate *stasis*, and the teachers gave a good deal of thought to it. Originally – in Hermagoras, it seems – the normal place to teach this technique was at the end of the course, after everything else. This was natural enough, for the arguments involved are not strictly to do with the question at issue, but with extraneous matters: the status of the court or the time at which the case is brought. Later theorists, however, found it convenient to teach it earlier, and there was a certain amount of controversy about where it belonged. Hermogenes has it after *pragmatikē*; in putting it earlier, I follow Sopatros. With minor differences, his *diairesis* is the same as Hermogenes'.[64]

His first instance is the case of the woman who has killed her husband as an adulterer.[65] She will need an advocate, for she

---

[63] εἰς δέον: cf. Aristophanes, *Clouds* 859 εἰς τὸ δέον ἀπώλεσα.
[64] Hermogenes 79ff Rabe.
[65] *RG* VIII.247ff; cf also ibid. 384–5, where the same case appears under another heading and the woman appears to speak for herself (384.29, 385.8), and

cannot speak for herself. The advocate's speech begins (i) with a *katastasis*, in which he praises the woman's chastity and enlarges on the value of domestic loyalty for the community at large and the 'democracy'. Then (ii) comes the 'demurrer': she has killed an adulterer, surely she should not even be tried, for she has only done what the laws allow. The *metalēpsis* which follows (iii) is the prosecutor's assertion that the law did not allow *the woman* to take action; this is an appeal to the letter of the law (*rhēton*), and may therefore be countered (iv) by an appeal to its spirit (*dianoia*). Other counter-measures are also possible: 'the law does not explicitly say whether husbands or wives may kill'; or again, 'where the result is the same, other differences do not matter' – sailors and sick men do not care by what means they come safely out of their troubles, so long as the relief comes. Again, it is the same for the adulterer whether a man or a woman exacts the penalty from him (v); and the importance of the act (*pēlikotēs*) rests not on the manner in which it is performed but on its appropriateness (vi). The *antithesis* which the defendant can now adduce (vii) is a counter-charge (*antenklēma*), showing that the adulterer deserves the fate. The prosecutor however has another shot in his locker – the second *metalēpsis* (viii) – and objects that the woman ought to have consulted the *dēmos* before taking the law into her own hands. But, she may answer, the law is perfectly clear (ix), and there was no need for consultation. The epilogue is an appeal to the jury to defend morality. What can be said here about adulterers is familiar to the pupil from his early exercises.[66]

Sopatros also gives us the prosecutor's speech. This begins (i) with a *katastasis* which has to make out that the husband has been a loyal and decent citizen and the wife impatient and hasty in treating his infidelity as she has. The demurrer (*paragraphikon*) (ii) is here the defendant's assertion that she should not be tried for killing an adulterer, and the *metalēpsis* that answers it (iii) makes the point that it was not appropriate for *her* to 'put in the sword'. The prosecution must then try to rebut the defendant's insistence on the spirit of the law, and this is done (iv) by an

the *protheōria* ('introduction') to [Liban.] *Decl.* 43. For the theme in general, see Bonner (1949) 119.

[66] 249.21: ἔχεις ἐκ τοῦ προγυμνάσματος ἅπαντας ἐναρμόσαι τοὺς τόπους.

argument from intention, pointing out that the lawgiver understood that it is the husband who is the sufferer in adultery, and it is his right therefore to exact the penalty. Moreover, even if one grants the defence point that the law leaves it vague who is to act, it remains true that the responsibility rests on the man's family, not on his wife, who has no connection of kinship with it. The *syllogismos*, (v) is the contrary of the defendant's; examples, parallels and general sentiments can be used to build up the argument that men and women are in a very different position in the matter. 'Importance' (vi) is easy: it is an intolerable thing for a woman so to fill her home with tragic disaster. The woman's counter-charge (vii) must now be answered; this is done (viii) by saying that she ought to have consulted others – her husband deserved to die, but at the hands of the public executioner. The epilogue appeals to the jury to punish a woman who has shown such contempt for the law.

Cases like this are distinguished by Sopatros from another type which depends on the 'law' that no one can be tried twice for the same offence. These necessarily involve another *stasis*, that of the original case (*euthydikia*). A typical instance is the case of the young man who has assaulted someone and is now disowned by his own father; the victim of the assault then prosecutes him for *hybris* (violent conduct), and he claims that he has already been tried and punished. The question is whether the disowning by the father counts as a punishment. The prosecutor has to develop the line that there has been no trial, and the father's action cannot count as one; indeed, the young man would probably have been disowned anyway, since his public conduct presumably only reflects the violence of his behaviour at home. Perhaps again it is all a trick, the father conniving at the son's escape from his deserts. The defendant must show himself to be a well-behaved youth, overwhelmed by his father's severity – which he feels far more acutely than any public trial – and convinced that his father will not take him back again. He must also press the point that the prosecution ought to have been brought before his father dismissed him from home. Sopatros, as often, gives hints for both speeches, no doubt because it was the practice in his school to have pupils perform against each other – surely the most effective and interesting method of teaching.[67]

7
Pragmatikē

Hermogenes and his successors used the term 'pragmatic', as a convenient heading under which to reckon deliberative speeches and certain particularly common types of exercise – claims to rewards, disputes about rewards, self-denunciations (*prosangeliai*) and accusations of 'unconstitutional proposals'.[68] There is perhaps not much rationale in this classification. One of its objects was certainly to bring deliberative oratory under the same system of instruction as forensic. Many of the most popular exercises in the schools were deliberative, especially the historical ones; and in real life the two genres are not easily separated, especially as many criminal trials had political overtones. But the addition of the other types of exercise seems unreasonable: they are mainly 'about the past', whereas the defining characteristic of deliberative oratory – and of the *pragmatikē stasis* in Hermogenes – is that it is 'about the future'. Reward and self-denunciation cases always imply something very like the provisions of a law – a fixed scale of qualifications for reward or of misfortunes that make life not worth living.

Hermogenes' account of the *pragmatikē*[69] is different in form from his discussion of other *staseis*. He makes a distinction – which is not a fundamental one – between cases depending on written laws and cases which do not: for example, if Cleon asks to be given the title Pythios after the victory at Pylos, no legal provision or enactment is involved. Apart from this, he contents himself with listing the 'heads of purpose' (*telika kephalaia*) and naming them as providing the principle of the *diairesis*. But this is of course not a *diairesis* in the sense in which he has been using the term, and the speaker has in fact to devise this for himself.

[67] Pernot (1981) 81f regards *antilogiai* as rather rare in Greek declamatory practice, but allows that the evidence is not strong. These pairs of speeches in Sopatros suggest that the practice was usual, which is what one might naturally expect.
[68] *RG* IV.226 (Syrianus).   [69] 76 Rabe.

That advice should be given 'according to the heads of purpose' is (as we have seen) traditional rhetorical teaching from the early days. In Hermogenes, there are six *kephalaia*: legality (*nomimon*); justice (*dikaion*); expediency (*sympheron*), subdivided into 'useful' and 'necessary'; possibility (*dynaton*), subdivided into 'not difficult' and 'difficult'; 'glory' (*endoxon*); and 'consequence' (*to ekbēsomenon*).

Sopatros works a number of examples; his *prosangeliai* are mostly 'figured', the speaker's real aim being different from the ostensible one. A clear example[70] is the case of the young man, disowned by his father, who 'denounces himself', in the knowledge that his father, as general, will have to administer the poison. In this case, what the boy really wants is to be taken back into the bosom of the family. The main theme is 'legality'. After the *katastasis*, which describes the young man's education, devotion to his family, and intolerable distress at being excluded from it, the speaker tackles (i) the first objection to his request: 'Disowned children are not granted this right by the law'. This is answered 'by objection' (*kat' enstasin*): 'Indeed they are, and more than anyone else, for it is a very dreadful thing to be disowned'. The second objection (ii) is that he is not unique; many young men have suffered this deprivation. The answer to this is to point out the special features of his plight: his father has acted arbitrarily without cause,[71] and there is no hope of his being restored. Moreover, men differ from one another in what they can tolerate, and this is why the law does not specify any particular misfortune but grants the right of self-denunciation to anyone who 'desires' it. Thirdly (iii), the father may say that he acted only to chasten his son. The reply is to ask what the offence was, and to point out that he had other means of redress – beatings, threats – and that, if the act had been merely chastisement, it should have been revoked before things came to the present pass. That the act is revocable (iv) is an obvious point; the answer is not only that the father is unlikely to relent, but that, even if he did, the son would continue to feel disgraced and insecure. The

[70] RG VIII.336. [71] RG VIII.337, 19.

past cannot be brought back. Finally (v), it is an objection to his request that the law does not command a man to give the poison to his sons.[72] The rebuttal (vi) is 'by definition': the young man is no longer his father's son, nor does the law prescribe to whom the general is to give the poison. An emotional epilogue closes the piece. The structure of this speech is thus very simple: the backbone is a series of *antitheseis*, each of which is answered. Such are most of Libanius' *prosangeliai*.

8
Staseis nomikai (*status legales*)

'Legal' issues never exist on their own; there is always an 'issue of reasoning' with them. But it was an important and characteristic part of rhetorical teaching to give instruction on how to debate the interpretation of laws. Indeed, philosophers could say that nothing showed the corruption of rhetoric better than its habit of 'transgressing laws by "letter and spirit"', saying that the spirit of law is different from the law itself'.[73]

Four types of *stasis nomikē* were usually recognized: 'letter and spirit' (*rhēton kai dianoia*); 'antinomy' or 'conflict of laws' (*antinomia*); 'amphiboly' or 'ambiguity' (*amphibolia*); and 'inference' or 'implication' (*syllogismos*).

(a) Hermogenes' type-example of 'letter and spirit' is the familiar case of the foreigner who went and fought on the walls of the city, though access to them was forbidden to all foreigners.[74] The *diairesis* is complex, made up partly of elements of 'definition' and partly from 'antitheticals'. The intention of the lawgiver and of the defendant are important points, and there is a good deal of discussion about the significance of the wording of the law: does it matter that it makes no mention of circumstances or intentions?

Sopatros' examples are more fully worked out. One of them

[72] Reading παισί for πατράσι at 339.9.
[73] Cf Olympiodorus, *In Gorgiam* 71.3 Westerink: ἡ... ῥητορικὴ διαφθείρει τὸν ἴδιον κανόνα· κανὼν δὲ αὐτῆς ὁ δικαστής· σπεύδει οὖν ἀπατῆσαι αὐτὸν ἐλεεινολογουμένη. ὡσαύτως καὶ νόμους παραβαίνει κατὰ ῥητὸν καὶ διάνοιαν λέγουσα ὅτι ἡ διάνοια ἄλλη ἐστὶ τοῦ νόμου. [74] Hermogenes 82–92 Rabe.

has its scene at Olympia.[75] The law (so it is said) lays down that a competitor who has entered for the games but fails to attend is not to be admitted again. A competitor, after entering, returns home to fight for his city, and wins the prize of valour. But he misses the festival, and tries to register a second time. Should he be allowed to do so?

The athlete's speech begins (i) with an elaborate *katastasis*, in which he defends his choice of life, and makes the point that athletics is the best training for war. The characteristic topic of the whole speech – 'letter and spirit' – comes next (ii). The 'letter' of the law is undoubtedly against the athlete, and so he has to counter it by interpreting its 'spirit'; this he does by arguing that it only applies to the same festival, and that it would be extremely inhumane if it failed to allow for exceptional circumstances; if someone fell ill in the course of the games, would he be debarred from competing again? The next move (iii) is a *metastasis*, in which the athlete asks to be forgiven because his motive was pity for his country, and justifies himself (*antistasis*) by the glories of his *aristeia*. The opponent (iv) can of course argue that the athlete's city would have survived without him; the answer (v) is that it would have been a disgrace to be aiming at an Olympic crown when the city faced slavery. Another 'antileptic' antithesis is however possible (vi): 'You ought to have competed first and fought the battle afterwards'. This is not difficult to refute (vii): it would have been too late. Again the opponent comes back (viii): you ought to have consulted the officials at the games. The answer (ix) is 'conjectural' (*stochastikē*): they might have forbidden me to go. And if they *had* agreed, the result would have been what it now is. The epilogue is grandiose: battle descriptions, an appeal to let the *aristeus* be also *Olympionikes*, a vision of his triumphal return.

The accuser's speech is quite different in tone. It is his part to be zealous for the law and to belittle the hero's achievement in battle. His *katastasis* (i) therefore tells of the acknowledged

[75] *RG* VIII.349ff. Olympia was a favoured setting: Apsines 235.3 Sp.–H., Sen. *Contr.* 5.3. Note also [Aeschines] *Epist.* 4.5–6, probably a work of the second century A.D., and very much in the tradition of the rhetorical schools.

validity of the Olympic laws, and represents the athlete's absence as an insult. He then proceeds to the various objections that the claimant can make: the contention (ii) that the prohibition applies only to the present contest may be answered (iii) by the suggestion that the law would have said that if it had meant it. Other arguments follow. The man should not have broken one law in order to keep another; his help to his country was not of great significance; and it is absurd of him to say that he could not have waited long enough to consult the proper authorities. The epilogue is a plea to maintain tradition.

(b) As an instance of *antinomia*, conflict of laws, I take the case in which a man rapes a blind man's daughter, and the blind man, hearing her scream, walks over a cliff; the rapist is then accused of causing his death. There are two versions of this in Sopatros, of which the second seems more coherent.[76]

There are two laws involved: one requiring a rapist to pay a fine of 10,000 drachmas, the other prescribing the death penalty for 'causing death'. The prosecution has the letter of the second law on its side, while the letter of the first favours the defence. So the accuser — whose speech is given first — repels the defence's insistence on the fine by discussing the spirit and intention of the law of rape, and then states his own requirement of literal observance of the homicide law, rebutting the defence's attempt to invalidate this by the appeal to spirit. The detail is interesting.

(i) The accuser's *katastasis* makes much of the blind man's dependence on his daughter and the horror of her sudden disappearance. The blind man wonders which way to turn; the girl's cries call the father to her aid. The 'legal *antitheseis*' follow. The rapist admits the offence and offers the fine (ii). The answer (iii) rests on interpreting the intention of the law: it applies to normal cases of rape, at festivals for example, not to aggravated cases which involve breaking other laws, as in the present instance. But the opponent may say, turning to the other law in the case, that it has no force here (iv): 'causing death' means

---

[76] *RG* VIII.362ff, 370ff; cf above, p. 35. The theme recalls the blind Oedipus led by his daughter Antigone and Karion's threat in Aristophanes (*Plutus* 69) to let the blind Ploutos fall off a precipice.

pushing someone over, or handing someone a sword or a drug, not letting a blind man fall over a precipice. 'Inference' (v) is one response to this: depriving a blind man of his guide is as bad as any of these. 'Lawgiver's intention' (vi) is another response: the law does not define ways of causing death, it leaves us to supply this for ourselves. 'Importance' and 'relative importance' (vii and viii) are also topics for this part of the speech. If it is said (ix) that the father was himself to blame, on the ground that he should have waited where he was, the answer (x) is that no father could be expected to stand still if he heard his daughter scream. And if the accused pleads (xi) that he did it for love, there are two ways of replying: (xii) the situation demanded pity, not love; and (xiii) if he really loved her, he should have asked her father for her hand. The epilogue attacks the accused as a violent criminal, relying on his wealth to buy him a way out of the consequences of his vicious act.[77] So how can he defend himself? His *katastasis* (i) aims at showing him as a mild and decent man, very much in love and anxious to have a wife. He snatched the girl from her father because he believed the father would never willingly let her go. His excuse is his passionate love. In arguing his case, he turns first (ii) to the point made by his opponent, that the law of rape prescribes a fine simply for the violence. He counters this (iii) by the usual appeal to the 'letter of the law': it makes no stipulation about the circumstances, but lays down the fine for rape in simple and absolute terms. He then deals (iv) with the objection made to his case on the ground of the law about 'causing death'. His answer to this (v) is 'by definition'; he did not provide the old man with his means of death. What he did was very far from that. But the girl may say (vi) 'My father wanted to rescue me'. The answer to this (vii) is, first, that the old man could not give much help; and, secondly, that love is an irresistible force, and lovers are as invincible as men possessed. 'But you should have asked her father' (viii); 'I was afraid he would refuse me' (ix). The epilogue takes what one might think a somewhat impudent line: the rapist asks to be allowed to pay his fine to provide a dowry for his bride, and offers

---

[77] We observe here also (cf ch. 2, p. 27) that the villain is characterized as rich.

to discuss with her the arrangements for her father's funeral, and even the inscription to be put on his tomb.

(c) Verbal ambiguity (*amphibolia, ambiguitas*) often comes into legal argument, and had long interested rhetoricians.[78] As Greek texts were normally written without word-divisions or punctuation, there was a particular risk, and the question whether a testator left his estate 'all to Leon' or 'to Pantaleon' (*panta Leonti* or *Pantaleonti*) was no doubt of a kind that actually occurred. The rhetors' examples[79] read more like grammarians' puzzles, but *diaireseis* were devised and taught. Hermogenes' model hinges on an accent: 'if a *hetaira* wears golden ornaments, *dēmosia estō*'. This means either 'let her become public property (*dēmosíā*)' or 'let them (i.e. the ornaments) become public property (*dēmósia*)'. We debate this as follows:

(i) Statement of literal meaning: 'The law commands that you should belong to the public'.

(ii) Second statement relying on the ambiguity: 'not me but the ornaments'.

(iii) 'Lawgiver's intention' is examined by both sides in accordance with their advantage: e.g. 'The lawgiver thought the offence deserved a penalty' *either* 'which was the greatest', *or* 'which was moderate, just as he laid down proportionate penalties in other offences'.

(iv) 'Including and included':[80] if the hetaira becomes public property, so will her gold ornaments; if they alone are confiscated, she is released.

(v) The *antithesis* follows immediately: it may be, for example, a counter-charge, the accuser arguing against the hetaira by means of commonplaces (*topikōs*).

(vi) This is followed by the *metalēpsis*: 'If she is a hetaira she has the special status of the profession in not being like free women or being thought worthy of the same privileges'; at the same time her advocate will rouse pity by professing her poverty or something of that sort.

(vii) *Quality* and *state of mind* as in other *staseis*. In this particular

---

[78] Aristotle, *Rhet.* 3.1407a31ff.
[79] Sopatros, *RG* VIII.377; *RG* IV.843ff; Hermogenes 90ff Rabe.
[80] περιέχον καὶ περιεχόμενον.

case, there is considerable opportunity for 'state of mind', since it is a question whether she has worn the ornaments in contempt of the law or simply in ignorance of it.

A different type of ambiguity is that found in oracles. In 480 B.C., the Athenians were told by Delphi that 'Wide-seeing Zeus gives wooden walls to Athena'.[81] The interpretation of this also can be made the subject of a *diairesis*. Sopatros offers one.[82] The *katastasis* (i) gives the story of the inquiry and the god's answer. Then (ii) comes the proposed interpretation of the wooden walls as triremes. The antithesis (iii) states that this is not what the god actually said; he ordered a wooden fortification for the acropolis, such as there had been in the past. The response is 'conjectural' (iv): the god did not mean this, for a wooden wall can be of no use to us if the sea is lost. In any case (v), such a fortification would be quite useless against a Persian siege; how could it stand up to fire or to siege-engines? A second antithesis (vi) follows: it would be a great labour to build the triremes. Answer (vii): that is not the question, what matters is whether we can defeat the barbarians by this means. The epilogue is at once an exhortation, an appeal to the gods, and a vision of the future, when the Athenians' wisdom in understanding the oracle will be famous the world over.

The application of the techniques of *diairesis* to problems like these has perhaps an additional interest; it offered a technique which could also be used for the purposes of scholarship and philosophy. It might be a worthwhile inquiry to see what traces of it could be found in the antiquarians, philosophers and theologians of late antiquity.

(d) Finally, *syllogismos*, 'inference' or 'implication'.[83] A playwright introduces the objects of his satire (*kōmōdoumenous*) on the stage in individually recognizable masks. Is he liable to the law that forbids 'satirizing by name'? This echo of an old tradition[84] concerning Aristophanes is also capable of treatment

---

[81] Herodotus 7.141.   [82] *RG* VIII.378.
[83] *RG* VIII.379.
[84] For the various traditions relating to the control of comic invective, see C. O. Brink, comm. on Horace, *Ars poetica* 283–4. Cf also *Ad Herennium* 1.14.24 for a Latin version, involving Accius and a mime actor.

by the *diairesis* technique.⁸⁵ It is very like a 'definition'; its main heads are (i) 'lawgiver's intention' – his aim was to diminish dissension and improve morals; (ii) 'importance' and (iii) 'relative importance' – it is actually worse to represent people in this sort of caricature than to mention them by name; (iv) 'antileptic' antithesis: 'I did it to chasten them', and (v) the reply: 'You could have done it in other ways.' The epilogue tries to show the feelings of the victims when they see the caricatures of themselves on the stage.

9

This type of teaching, with its concentration on *staseis* and appropriate *diaireseis*, was not to everybody's taste. It certainly needed much supplementation. The teacher of declamation could not take for granted that his pupils had mastered all the subordinate skills which they needed. Making a *diairesis* did not exempt one from knowing how to compose *prooimia*, narratives and epilogues, nor from understanding how epicheiremes and examples were to be put together. We have seen that the *progymnasmata* – *ēthopoiia*, *thesis*, *locus communis*, comparison, for example – play a part in declamation; all this had to be understood and, as it were, constantly revised. It is noticeable that Sopatros, whose manual is so much more detailed than Hermogenes', often spends time and trouble on an expansive treatment of *prooimia*, *katastaseis* and examples, clearly for pedagogic reasons. Nor of course could the skills of style be assumed. Here, we find different emphases in different teachers. Sopatros, though his models are usually in correct Attic, does not give the impression of being particularly concerned with the *mimēsis* of the classical models, though he often uses tags from Demosthenes; there is nothing in him like the recommendation we find in ps.-Dionysius about studying the special vocabulary of Aristophanes, Eupolis or Antiphon.⁸⁶ On the whole, Sopatros confines himself to a general comment on the emotional tone required by the exercise;

---

⁸⁵ *RG* VIII.383ff, taking the fuller version of the text in C [see Preface]. Sopatros' theme is mentioned elsewhere in the rhetors: Hermogenes 88 Rabe, *RG* IV.234.
⁸⁶ *Ars rhetorica*, p. 365 Usener–Radermacher.

Alcibiades has to be proud and splendid in his speech, a poor man needs to be modest and humble.[87] Only occasionally do we find a comment on sentence-structure, usually when emotion dictates the breakdown of the normal periodic style into short phrases or exclamations.[88] Of the text-books which do go further, and which help to correct the impression of an obsessive concern with *diairesis* which we get from Hermogenes' *On Staseis* and his commentators, the most interesting is to be found in the *Art of Rhetoric* of ps.-Dionysius. The two small treatises on the criticism of declamation are of unknown date, perhaps late second or third century.[89] They make some important points, clearly directed against rival teachers more than against unsatisfactory pupils. Two principles may be singled out.

(i) For this rhetor, character (*ēthos*) is of central significance. It is not just an incidental, to be indicated by odd remarks here and there; it must be woven into the whole texture of the speech. The declaimer needs to envisage his personages clearly and make sure that his argument chimes with them throughout. The battle is one of character as much as of fact. So far, teachers like Sopatros would not dissent. But when ps.-Dionysius goes on to urge that a good declamation requires also a 'philosophical *ēthos*', that is to say a general tendency to promote virtue, he is clearly going beyond what the mere technical rhetor would agree to, and is taking up a position as a moral educator. We should, I take it, assume a considerable range of opinions on this issue; it is at the heart of the continuing educational debate of antiquity between the rhetors and the philosophers.

(ii) Ps.-Dionysius' other important point concerns order and proportion. It is clearly important to distinguish a *diairesis* into 'headings' (*kephalaia*) from the plan of an actual speech. Sopatros does not do this and gives the impression that the pupil will get

[87] Sopatros has a very limited range of descriptive terms for stylistic tone, and makes no use of the refined terminology of Hermogenes' *ideai*: we find only such terms as (e.g.) πομπεία ('magnificence'), μεγαληγορία ('grandeur'), βαρύτης ('indignation'), φιλοτιμία ('pride', 'ambitiousness').

[88] E.g. *RG* VIII.161.21ff: μετὰ ταῦτα τοὺς ἐπιλόγους θήσεις, συνάψας εὐθὺς κομματικῶς ('then you should add the epilogue, connecting it immediately with short phrases'). [89] See ch. 1, n. 26.

full marks if he follows the *diairesis* in the order given. Ps.-Dionysius will have none of this.[90] Setting out the *kephalaia* in such a way is no better than writing out the letters in the order of the alphabet instead of using them to make words. What is vital is to see what is needed in a particular case, to arrange the strong argument so as to conceal the weak, and to anticipate opponents' arguments in a sophisticated and persuasive manner. Similarly with the traditional 'parts of a speech'.[91] They are not always to be written up exactly as the text-books say. Narrative in particular may be very short, or even unnecessary: 'narratives of battle exploits are ludicrous', and when *aristeis* and generals dispute for prizes they do not have to tell the whole story of the war. Ps.-Dionysius claims to be more practical than most, and pointedly contrasts 'sophists' lectures' with 'real rhetoric'.[92] This claim is in part justified; he has sensible remarks to make on the foolishness of traditional arguments which have no bearing on the issue to be tried. But his archaism, his strong moral line, and his aesthetic and literary approach make it clear that the main thrust of his effort is to contribute to a liberal education rather than to teach techniques.

[90] *Ars rhetorica*, p. 363 Usener–Radermacher.
[91] Ibid. 367ff.
[92] Ibid. 371, 27.

4
Performers and occasions

Δότε μοι σῶμα καὶ μελετήσομαι.
'Give me a body and I will declaim!'
                                    Polemon of Laodicea

I

Declamations might be taught in school, delivered in public, or written down for distant or future admiration. These functions complemented one another; the teacher won pupils by giving a good performance, the literary man sought from posterity that praise which the tastelessness of his audiences denied in his lifetime. In this chapter, I look at some of the evidence – mostly anecdotal – for these various activities. What did rhetors really do? What were they like?

Even the wealthiest and most ambitious took pupils, though they did not, like their inferiors, have to spend their days entirely in the company of schoolboys. Aristides, by no means a born teacher, sometimes took fees.[1] Lollianus, the great Ephesian sophist who held the chair of rhetoric at Athens[2] and was noted also for his legal expertise, not only taught declamation by example and exercise but gave theoretical instruction – in other words, lectures on the kinds of topics that Hermogenes, Apsines and Minucianus professed.[3] Herodes Atticus, a man of immense wealth and repute, both gave public lectures and provided extra

---

[1] Philostratus, *VS* 605.
[2] Ibid. 526, Bowersock (1969) 18, 57. 'Chair' is no anachronism: the *thronos* or *cathedra* from which the teacher spoke in class symbolized his office, and 'professorial' appointments were made in many cities, funded at public expense: see H. I. Marrou, *Histoire de l'éducation dans l'antiquité* (ed. 2, Paris 1950), Troisième Partie, ch. 8, 'L'état romain et l'éducation'.
[3] In Philostratus' words (loc. cit.): οὐ μελετηρὰς μόνον [sc. συνουσίας] ἀλλὰ καὶ διδασκαλικὰς παρέχων.

Performers and occasions

classes for select pupils, a sort of seminar by special admission.[4] But among Philostratus' anecdotes, it is the story of Proclus of Naucratis[5] that gives the most vivid impression of the successful teacher's life. Proclus came to Athens, we are told, to escape disorder in his native city; he was a rich man, and he increased his wealth by trade. Philostratus was among his pupils:

The traditions of declamation in this man's school were as follows. Anyone who paid a single sum of a hundred drachmas[6] was permitted to attend lectures in perpetuity. There was a library at Proclus' home, to which the audiences had access to supplement the lecture. To prevent us from hissing or mocking one another — as often happens in sophists' lectures — we were called in all together and then sat in groups, the young boys and their attendants in the centre, and the older boys by themselves. He very rarely gave a *dialexis*,[7] but when he did it was in the manner of Hippias and Gorgias.[8] The declamation which had been announced in the course of the previous day was now brought up. At the age of ninety, he had a better memory than Simonides;[9] his style was natural, his way of piling on thoughts recalled Adrian.

2

To a certain extent, the procedures of the schools were extended to public performance. In any case, teaching was often done in public places: when Hippodromos of Thessaly first visited

---

[4] Philostratus, *VS* 585ff. On Herodes (consul in 143) see Bowersock (1969) 92–100, and esp. the major study of P. Graindor, *Un milliardaire antique: Hérode Atticus et sa famille* (Paris 1930).

[5] Philostratus, *VS* 604. Naucratis, the site of a Milesian 'factory' in Egypt from the seventh century B.C., experienced a brief period of intellectual distinction under the Antonines, and produced noted scholars and scientists: Pollux, Apollonius, Athenaeus, Ptolemy (Bowersock [1969] 20).

[6] This is a very small fee. Damianus paid 10,000 drachmas to Aristides and Adrian, Scopelianus varied fees according to pupils' means. Proclus was himself a pupil of Adrian. The willingness to take pupils of talent who had little means is an interesting phenomenon.

[7] I.e. an informal preliminary talk (Lat. *sermo*); see below, p. 77.

[8] This suggests 'imitation' of the somewhat crude style of the early sophists, heavily antithetical and with considerable poetic colour.

[9] Simonides and the art of memory: Cic. *De oratore* 2.351ff. Simonides was known as the inventor of mnemonics in Hellenistic and later times. The story was that he remembered where everyone had sat at Scopas' banquet, and so was able to help identify the bodies when the roof fell in (Blum [1969] 41ff).

Smyrna, and wanted to hear something of Ionian rhetoric, 'he noticed a temple and children's attendants sitting near it, with slaves accompanying them, carrying loads of books in satchels;[10] he therefore concluded that some famous man was giving a lesson within'.[11] Temples were also among the buildings used for more public exhibitions, along with theatres, council chambers and sometimes specially built lecture-halls.[12] Aristides[13] performs in the council chamber at Cyzicus, and subsequently gives the same speech at a festival (*panēgyris*). At Smyrna he is kept out of the council chamber till midday by a rival already in possession, but declaims with success in the afternoon. The lecture-halls could be large and splendid: Lucian[14] – not without irony – describes a particularly fine one, which echoes like a cavern with the speaker's lingering clausulae and distracts the audience with its magnificent decoration. Audiences could be large, perhaps a thousand or more, for there would not only be the young, but all the older people who wanted to keep alive or recapture the excitements of their youth. A visit from a well-known sophist from abroad was a special pleasure. Aristides is again in Smyrna:[15]

Before I even entered the city, there were people coming to meet me because they had heard about me, the most distinguished of the young men were giving themselves to me, and there was already a definite plan for a lecture. The invitation list was being arranged. Now there was a little Egyptian who had bounced into town, corrupted some of the councillors and given some of the ordinary people the impression that he would play a part in public affairs and spend his money on certain marvellous acts of public generosity. Well, into the theatre he runs, in no sort of order, and the whole town is disgraced. I knew nothing about this till late, because I was at home engaged in discussion

[10] ἐν πήραις: cf Hor. *Sat.* 1.6.74 laevo suspensi loculos tabulamque lacerto.
[11] Philostratus, *VS* 618.
[12] On *akroatēria*, see B. P. Hillyard, comm. on Plutarch, *De audiendo* (Arno Press, New York 1981), on 45F; L. Robert, *Études anatoliennes* (Paris 1937) 76–81.
[13] *Or.* 51.16, 51.38.
[14] In *Peri tou Oikou* (*De domo*), 1.58ff Macleod. Cf Bompaire (1958) 713f. The elaborate paintings are a significant reminder that sophistic oratory was delivered in urban settings rich in visual art, to which it constantly alludes and responds.
[15] *Or.* 51, 29–34.

with my friends. He was just about to enter the Odeion by the Harbour and was organizing a lecture there, either under the terms of a decree or in some other circumstances – I don't know; but I had a dream. I dreamed that I saw the sun rising over the Agora, and I had on my lips the words 'Aristides will declaim to-day in the Council Chamber at the fourth hour'. As I spoke and heard these words, I woke up; so I wondered whether it was a dream or a waking experience. I called those friends who were on hand, and told them the orders. An advertisement was put out (the time mentioned in the dream was approaching) and we were there hard on its heels. Despite the fact that my appearance was impromptu, and most people knew nothing about it, the Council Chamber was so full that you could see nothing but human faces – and you couldn't have thrust your hand between. The noise and the good will, or rather (to tell the truth) the enthusiasm, were so universal that there was no-one to be seen sitting down either during my preliminary speech or when I stood up and declaimed. From the very first word they stood there, keyed up, joyful, amazed.... when I had left the Council Chamber and was in the bath, I was told that a certain person, having given two days' notice, had got together in the Odeion on that day a total audience of – seventeen![16]

3

Aristides' 'preliminary speech' – here called *proagōn* – which he delivered sitting down, is a regular feature of sophistic exhibition. It was often called *dialexis*, *prolalia* or just *lalia*, names which indicate that it was meant to be informal, a sort of conversational chat, quite distinct from the formal rhetorical *logos*. It was usually spoken while sitting down, though Scopelianus[17] at least sometimes stood up for it, and then delivered it in a more vigorous fashion. We must infer that usually the *dialexis* was comparatively quiet in manner, unaccompanied by the sometimes violent gestures of the orator in full flood. It was ordinarily a polite introduction, courteous to the audience, not necessarily modest but at least disarming. It was used not only as a preface to a performance of declamation but also before formal encomia;

[16] In Liban. *Epist.* 405, Libanius' first appearance as a teacher produces an audience of 'seventeen', but as soon as his quality is perceived 'the nations come pouring in'. This, with the passage in Aristides, suggests that 'seventeen' is a traditionally derisory number.   [17] Philostratus, *VS* 519.

and it differed from both these in style and in content. It was customary to compose it in syntactically simpler form, with short sentences and no periodic structure. This was *apheles logos*, not *politikos logos*.[18] It dealt in anecdotes, elaborate comparisons,[19] mythology and witty allusions to the classics. It did not deal in argument. Some thought it childish;[20] others devoted a good deal of care to it. Indeed, it developed into something of an art-form itself: a number of Lucian's pieces[21] were composed as *laliai*, and seem to have constituted complete performances. And it had of course affiliation – as the name *dialexis* suggests – with the 'conversational' forms of popular philosophy. Some of Plutarch's moral treatises have unmistakable signs of this form; and in Maximus of Tyre we see it developed into a sort of philosophical essay with a measure of serious intent. It is, however, at the very end of our tradition, in Choricius, that we find the most elegant examples of the declaimer's *dialexis*.[22] In some of these, problems of declamation itself are discussed. For example:[23]

Philip's boy, Alexander – for Philip's he was, even if he wished to be thought a child of Zeus – was moulded by many a sculptor, and depicted by many a painter. Most of their works he did not much praise, whether the medium was colour or bronze, because they represented some features of him but not others. But when he saw Lysippus' image of him, Alexander was pleased. Philip's Alexander had a quick, virile, proud and fearless character; Lysippus' Alexander had it too. He therefore bade the others take other models, and entrusted himself to

[18] On this distinction see esp. the *Ars rhetorica* attributed to Aristides (ed. W. Schmid, 1926), of which one book is devoted to each of the two main types of writing.

[19] Philostratus (*VS* 528) notes with particular admiration Marcus of Byzantium's comparison of the art of the sophist to a rainbow. The elaborate comparisons with which Plutarch, for example, often begins a moral discourse are part of this tradition. See also the advice in Menander Rhetor 388–94 Sp., with Russell and Wilson's comm., pp. 294ff.

[20] Antiochus of Aegae, *VS* 569.

[21] E.g. *Hippias, Dionysus, Heracles, Electrum, Gallus, Somnium, Dipsades, Herodotus, Zeuxis, Harmonides*.

[22] Richtsteig (*Prolegomena*, p. v) notes that the preservation of these *dialexeis* suggests that Choricius' works were put together from his own collection, perhaps by an immediate pupil.   [23] *Dialexis* 21, p. 382 F.–R.

Lysippus alone. So the Sicyonian made a good portrait of the man of Macedon; and similarly Timomachus did Medea, Aeetes' daughter, in a mixture of love and anger, the one for the children, the other for Jason, yet not in equal measure, for her love of her children took second place to her jealousy, and she was more wife than mother. You can hear her say:

> I understand what evils I shall do,
> But Jason is more powerful than my counsels.[24]

It would be wrong of me, I am sure, when I am telling you about sculpture and painters, to pass over in silence Myron's cow. This work was such that it was no vain boast to make it say: 'If a cow sees me, she will low; if a bull, he will mount me; if a cowman, he will drive me to the herd'.[25] Well, let Myron and Lysippus and others who share their pursuits take pride in their art; a man whose study is the tongue must use this to mimic whatever he fashions. Let it not be in vain that comedy calls the tongue a ball,[26] because it is mobile and easily turned wherever one will.

History, poetry, art-history; a fanciful comparison; and a hint of the versatility expected of the declaimer: content and style are typical of the *dialexis*.

4

After the *dialexis*, the sophist would probably invite proposals from the audience for his principal theme. If several were put forward, they might vote on it.[27] This willingness to 'answer questions' goes back to Gorgias and the early sophists. However elaborate the verbal art – and we must recall that, in the Roman period, all these exercises were carried out in a language well removed from the vernacular – skill in improvisation remained one of the most highly valued qualities. It naturally seemed wonderful that anyone should be able to speak Demosthenic Greek on the spur of the moment. Of course, not everyone had the facility in equal degree. Some speakers stood up and

---

[24] Euripides, *Medea* 1066–7: the text of Euripides has 'anger' (θυμός) where Choricius writes 'Jason'.
[25] See *Anth. Pal.* 9.730.
[26] Cf Aristophanes, *Frogs* 892, *Clouds* 792.
[27] There are standard expressions for the 'preferred' or 'desired' subject which was voted in: it was ἡ προκριθεῖσα (or σπουδασθεῖσα) ὑπόθεσις.

responded to the question put from the floor without further delay. Others took a short time to deliberate; this was the practice, for example, of the Syrian Isaeus, known to Juvenal for his fluency.[28] Others again took till next day: such was Aristides' usual practice,[29] which he maintained even before the emperor Marcus:

'When shall I hear you?' said the emperor.
'Propose the theme today', said Aristides, 'and hear it tomorrow: I belong to the perfectionists, not to the vomiters.'[30]

Not only perfectionists, but the less quick-witted naturally chose this way: Glycera in Aristaenetus complains that Strepsiades works at his speeches all night, gestures with his hands, and mutters to himself. Why, she asks, did such a man have to marry?[31]

We need not suppose that the 'improvisation' was always genuine. The themes were familiar, and the proposal from the floor could be easily stage-managed. But one of the consequences of the importance attached to such readiness was that sophists were not supposed to give exactly the same speech twice. It was very bad form to repeat yourself verbatim. If a speech had been circulated in writing, it could not then be used in performance; and circulation could happen without the author's knowledge, if eager audiences pooled their notes, or someone introduced a shorthand writer.[32] A story in Philostratus[33] illustrates the dangers. Philagros of Cilicia, a rather arrogant pupil of Herodes, was giving a performance at Athens. His *dialexis* was incoherent and childish – it included a lament for his own wife – and the audience had plotted to play a trick on him when he gave his actual declamation. They deliberately suggested to him a subject

---

[28] *VS* 514, Juv. 3.74.

[29] *Or.* 50.30: the god advised it, but (*Or.* 50.18) Aristides' first public performance seems to have been more or less impromptu.

[30] *VS* 583: οὐ γάρ ἐσμεν τῶν ἐμούντων ἀλλὰ τῶν ἀκριβούντων. Cf Liban. *Decl.* 27.8, and (in a somewhat different context) Cic. *Ad fam.* 12.2 where the drunken Antony is said to have seemed *vomere suo more, non dicere.*

[31] Aristaenetus, *Epistles* 2.3.

[32] Pooling notes: Liban. *Or.* 3.17. Shorthand: Eunapius 469, where we hear of shorthand writers sent for from the law-courts. Kennedy (1983) 15 gives some later evidence. [33] *VS* 579.

which they knew he had already treated in Asia. It was called 'The Alliance of the Uninvited'; it may have been based on an episode in Thucydides, where Alcibiades rejects a proffer of aid from the Argives.[34] Texts had reached Athens; and when Philagros, all unsuspecting, began to repeat his speech just as he had given it before, the audience chanted it back at him as he spoke.

Stories like this make one wonder about the relationship of the texts we have to the speeches actually declaimed. Do we possess pieces that we could chant back at their authors? The great variation in scale and treatment of the extant speeches engenders great doubt. We have evidence of very diverse kinds. Polemon, for example, had an immense reputation in antiquity for the vigour of his declamations. He was, it is well known, a bizarre personality.[35] A sick man, he would arrive at the theatre in a litter and apparently declaimed from his chair; but he would jump up, despite his frailty, at every high point of the theme, smiling with self-approbation at his rhythmical clausulae, displaying both ease of expression and a proud bearing 'like the well-fed stallion in Homer', that gallops boldly over the plain in search of the mares. His actual style is traditionally described by the word *rhoizos*, the 'rush' of stream or wind or wings.[36] One would not guess this from the short, dense and sober extant declamations about Marathon. The pieces attributed to Adrian of Tyre and to Lesbonax are also surprisingly short and undramatic. In all this, do we have summaries rather than full transcriptions? The actual performances can hardly have been so short. By contrast, Libanius and Choricius left very long, full and carefully polished speeches. So, in an earlier age, did the professed perfectionist Aristides. Some at least of these are models for future students, longer and more elaborate than would be required for any particular occasion, storehouses of technique and felicitous wording. There is nothing surprising in this; orators did the same, and the surviving speeches of Demosthenes and Cicero are often

[34] Thuc. 8.86.   [35] *VS* 537–8.
[36] Philostratus, *VS* 589: cf Russell and Wilson on Menander Rhetor, 386.30 Sp.

obviously different from anything that could actually have been said. In any case, we are dealing with a form of composition in which delivery and histrionic technique were of supreme importance. These men were actors: one day Persian kings – Scopelianus was admired for the way he 'shook' (*eseieto*) in trying to represent barbarian arrogance and emotion[37] – the next day solemn Spartans, misanthropic peasants or crippled veterans. It all took a lot of energy: Polemon admonishes a colleague whom he finds buying sprats and sausages for dinner; no-one, he pointed out, could hope to reproduce the pride and spirit of Darius and Xerxes on such a diet.[38] Critics often comment on the importance of *hypokrisis* (delivery),[39] and ridicule its exaggerations: and there is a certain amount of internal evidence, especially in Libanius, which enables us to imagine what a dramatic rendering of declamation might be like. *Ethopoiiai* demand a change of tone; so do objections and answers. We find references, equivalent to stage-directions, to raising the voice or to the weak and feeble utterance of an unhappy father.[40] But it would be a mistake to exaggerate the degree of illusion expected by the audience. The personality of the sophist himself was, it seems, more important; his dress and manners are often noted, neat appearance or conspicuous extravagance being liked, and plebeian roughness tolerated only as an eccentricity. They neither dressed up for the part they were taking nor much modified their Attic language to give the impression of barbarian or Spartan colour.[41] Nevertheless, the element of drama was there, and Choricius in particular consciously relates his art to that of the stage. We have from his hand two opposing declamations[42] concerning the young *aristeus* who claims as his prize the right to marry the pretty

---

[37] *VS* 520.   [38] *VS* 541.

[39] Lucian, *De saltatione* 65 says that *hypokrisis* is equally important for dancers and for rhetors, especially in *meletai*: 'We praise nothing so much in them as resemblance to the personages in their speeches – *aristeis*, tyrannicides or farmers'.

[40] At Liban. *Decl.* 31.37 the miser bawls at the lawgiver's tomb; at 32.50 the prosecutor is imagined raising his voice to the prostitute; at 33.36 the poor old father's voice is enfeebled.

[41] It sometimes appears as if bold metaphors or personifications were thought characteristic of barbarians: [Longin.] *De subl.* 4.7, [Dion. Hal.] *Ars* p. 378 Usener–Radermacher.   [42] *Decl.* 5 and 6.

girl he loves against the wishes of his father, who has determined on a wealthy but not so well-favoured bride for him. The *theōria* to the young man's speech[43] asserts that the speaker himself is young, and happily relinquishes the part of the old miser to someone of more appropriate character and age. The *theōria* to the miser's speech[44] then admits that the speaker is neither miserly nor a lover of money, nor even a father; his imitation of these qualities is therefore a matter of art, not nature. So a young speaker does both pieces, to one of which he is better suited than to the other. The natural conclusion has always been drawn, that this is a youthful work of Choricius. The *dialexis*[45] which is transmitted with these pieces and clearly refers to them discusses the impersonation involved.

You have, I have no doubt, been spectators of choruses in the festival of Dionysus, and I am sure you have seen a dancer charming the stage at one time with masculine figures, dancing the Thessalian or the Amazon's boy[46] or some other man, and at another time skilfully representing Briseis or Phaedra in love, and trying to persuade the audience not that he is representing something, but that he really *is* what he allegedly represents. Homer dances thus in his poems. Or don't you see that the poet appears to be whatever he wants? He certainly draws *my* imagination with him, and I fancy myself actually seeing in person any character he impersonates, the boy from Aetolia or the old man of Pylos[47] or in general any Achaean or any one of the enemies of the Greeks – whether it is the Muses who inspired him thus, or the Muses too are a fiction and it is an advantage of nature; at all events I admire his power and would dearly love to have something like it myself! However, Homer's tongue is versatile and full of grace, readily adaptable to any character; but I think *I* for my part had better seek out Athena and her goddess' wand, by which she often changed Odysseus' looks, so that she can make me appear an old man, now that I come before you to imitate that time of life.

I expect you remember the old miser, whose son fell in love with a poor girl, she being fair of face, while the father wished to marry him to a maiden who had no beauty, she being rich. Well, if you

[43] P. 226 F.–R.
[44] P. 253 F.–R.
[45] *Dialexis* 12, p. 248 F.–R.
[46] Achilles and Hippolytus.
[47] Diomedes and Nestor.

remember him, he makes our present performance. So I ought to have been old, and I ought to have been avaricious; for the representation of a speech is more vivid when the speaker is of the same age and character as the person whom he has invented.

Nevertheless, I don't believe I do need either of these additional qualifications, if you will only accord the old man as much good will as you did to the son the other day. In truth, my dear friends, it seemed absurd that, having fought on behalf of a young man and a pretty girl, I should then abandon to their fate an elderly man and a maiden with no great share of good looks. Yet it is a greater excellence of speech to make what is not beautiful appear so. A painter may contrive forms as they are, for that is his work, but an orator is allowed by his art to conceal what is ugly, be it persons or things.

5

I return in conclusion to the second century, to a story from Philostratus which, perhaps more than any other, encapsulates the tone and ambitions of the great declaimers and their audiences.[48]

Alexander 'Peloplaton', a native of Cilician Seleucia and a great traveller, passed through Athens on his way back from seeing the Emperor Marcus in Pannonia — he had been appointed Greek secretary (*ab epistulis graecis*)[49] — and agreed to give an exhibition of extempore speaking. We are to imagine a summer day, with the audience assembled 'in the theatre in the Ceramicus, which is called the Agrippeion'.[50] Herodes Atticus, now in retirement at Marathon, has promised to attend Alexander's performance, and to bring with him all his 'Hellenes'.[51] But the day wore on, and he did not come. The suspicious audience thought the delay was a trick, and Alexander was obliged to begin without waiting for his distinguished auditor. So he appeared;

---

[48] *VS* 571–4.
[49] Sophists often held posts of this kind; so also Maximus of Aegae (Bowersock [1969] 19). See Bowie (1982) 41ff.
[50] The Agrippeion is the Agora; it is not clear just why Philostratus names the Ceramicus. See Bowersock (1969) 17 n. 3.
[51] The use of *Hellēnes* or *Hellēnikon* for groups of persons of literary education, or pupils in a rhetor's school, reflects the 'nationalist' flavour of the sophists, who saw themselves in a very special sense as custodians of the heritage of classical Hellas.

Performers and occasions

he was a handsome man – curly beard, large eyes, white teeth, well-shaped nose. He was also so well turned out (*eustalēs*), that even before he spoke an appreciative murmur[52] ran through the audience. His *dialexis* dealt, as was proper, with the glories of Athens. He then asked for proposals for his main subject. The theme which was voted in – 'the winning *hypothesis*' – was a fairly familiar one:[53] 'advice to the Scythians to resume nomadic life because settling in cities has caused disease among them'. This is an example of a deliberative speech in favour of 'making a move' (*metoikein*): we know of other declamation examples – Lydians want to move because Pactolus has stopped flowing gold, Egyptians because the Nile fails, Sicilians because of earthquakes and volcanoes[54] – and indeed of poetical versions.[55] Add a prosecution of the original proposer of an urban life and we have a *controversia*. So it is well within a standard tradition. It also has an obvious moral aspect: town life versus country life, the primitivistic topic of the superiority of the Scythians of the steppes.[56] Alexander paused; then he jumped up 'with a joyful face, like one bringing good news to his hearers'. He was well advanced in his speech before Herodes and his party made their ostentatious entrance; but even this did not stem his flow. He made a graceful compliment to the great man, and asked him whether he would like to hear the theme which was under discussion or to propose another one himself. Herodes left it to the audience; they were for going on with 'The Scythians'. So Alexander went back over his speech, expressing the identical

[52] βόμβος presumably means 'murmur' or 'frisson'; but Suet. *Nero* 20 suggests that it just might be a kind of clapping or beating with the hands: bombos et imbrices et testas... plausuum genera. Here the last two are certainly hand-claps, named from the way in which the hands are held (hollow or flat, like the two different sorts of tile) and there are thus some grounds for thinking that *bombi* are the same kind of thing.
[53] Apsines 228, 230, 233 Sp.–H.
[54] Hermogenes 110, 2ff Rabe.
[55] Hor. *Odes* 1.7 and *Epodes* 16 may be adduced as examples.
[56] Cf Hor. *Odes* 3.24.9, campestres melius Scythae. For the theme in general, see Lovejoy and Boas (1935), Index, s.v. Scythians. Its popularity in the Second Sophistic is attested also by Lucian's 'Scythian' discourses (*Toxaris, Scytha, Anacharsis*), lately studied as a group by E. Steindl (*Luciani Scytharum colloquia* [1970], with his earlier articles cited there [p. vi]).

arguments in completely different words. This virtuosity was much admired, and evidently long remembered, for Philostratus gives us some quotations. The first version had contained the *sententia* 'Even water sickens when it stands still'.[57] The second version, given in Herodes' presence, was 'Even among waters, those that wander are sweeter'.[58] What Alexander did was to turn his *paradeigma* inside out, but in both ways making the point that being on the move is healthier than being at rest. His epilogue was particularly striking: he described the stifling heat of the city, and finally cried out 'Open the gates, I need to breathe!'

Herodes' own tastes were more sober and classical, but he would not let his pupils disparage Alexander too much, and, when it was his turn to declaim in Alexander's presence, he evidently cast off some of his usual restraint. Presumably he wanted to show that this more exuberant style was really quite easy. So his *dialexis* was full of elaborate rhythmical effects. The audience asked for a 'Sicilian' subject which demanded emotional power: 'The wounded Athenians at Syracuse ask their comrades to kill them rather than abandon them'. Herodes rose to the occasion. He had tears in his eyes when he cried out 'Nicias, father, as you hope to see Athens...!'[59]

[57] ἑστὸς καὶ τὸ ὕδωρ νοσεῖ. Not an original idea, but perhaps one current in declamation: note Ovid, *Epist. ex Ponto* 1.5.5–6: cernis...ut capiant vitium ni moveantur aquae.
[58] καὶ ὑδάτων ἡδίω τὰ πλανώμενα.
[59] Ναὶ Νικία, ναὶ πάτερ, οὕτως Ἀθήνας ἴδοις. Theme is from Thuc. 7.75.

5
Character and characters

'Ὡς εἰπεῖν τῷ ῥήτορι μόνος ὁ τοῦ ἤθους ἀγών ἐστιν.
'To all intents and purposes, the conflict of character is the rhetor's only conflict.'
                        Ps.-Dionysius, *Art of Rhetoric*

I

The importance of character (*ēthos*) in oratory was very familiar both to the Attic orators and to the early teachers of rhetoric.[1] It was important in three ways.

First, the speaker had to project a sympathetic image of himself. He needed to seem likable and – even more important – trustworthy.

Secondly, in order to ensure that he was really making the desired impression, he had to identify and study the specific qualities of his audience – age, interests, and nationality as well as what we should call qualities of character. He had to know, for example, how they would respond to pleas based on patriotism or self-interest.

Thirdly, he had to represent the characters of his opponents, and of other people appearing in his story, in such a way as to make his narrative plausible and make sure that it was understood as he wanted it to be.

Declamation, because it was a toy model of oratory, had the same concerns, but on a different level. For one thing, the declaimer has to invent his character. He does not stand forth as a real person with obvious characteristics which can be seen by all. Hermogenes significantly lists the creation of a distinct *ēthos* in the speaker as the first criterion to be fulfilled. if the case is to 'hang together'.[2] Secondly: an impersonated speaker and an

---

[1] See esp. W. Süss (1910), an illuminating and important book.
[2] 32f Rabe.

imaginary audience ('imaginary' because the audience actually present is judging not the case but the performance) not only impose new problems but permit new liberties. It was possible for the declaimer to give the speaker a personality which would have been wholly unsympathetic in real life. He could put on stage, as it were, a miser or a 'morose' old misanthropist (*dyskolos*) with whom no one could seriously sympathize, instead of a person like the real aggrieved husband and the real frustrated invalid whom we find in Lysias.[3] It was even possible to make unflattering assumptions about the audience, which would be impossible in real life, for example by assuming that they cared for nothing but money.[4] Similarly, some quite trivial characteristic – talkativeness or an obsessive dislike of noise – could appear in declamation not as an incidental but as a mainspring of the plot. When these potentialities of declamation are exploited it becomes a caricature of oratory. Its educational usefulness takes second place to its amusement value; there is no pill inside the sugar coating – unless indeed one adopts the line taken by Ps.-Dionysius, giving the primary rôle not to rhetorical technique but to the morally educative feature of a 'philosophical' tendency. Ps.-Dionysius' *philosophon ēthos* may well have been devised in response to the type of comic declamation that we see at its height in Libanius, but which probably existed at a much earlier date.[5]

2

This tendency led to a great extension of the rôle of the narrative – or, to be more exact, the *katastasis*, this being the regular term for the selective and admittedly angled narration by which the speaker laid the foundations of his case.[6] This is

[3] Compare characters like those of Liban. *Decl.* 30 (the 'envious man', φθονερός), 31 or 32 with the characterization in Lysias, *Or.* 1 (deceived husband) or 34 (invalid).

[4] Liban. *Decl.* 33.5.

[5] See ch. 1, n. 26 and ch. 3, n. 89, and the passage of Lucian cited in ch. 4, n. 39, which offers evidence for 'comic' character declamation in the second century.

[6] *Katastasis* is not an easy term. It is not always distinguished from *diēgēsis* ('narrative') – e.g. *RG* v.384 (Planudes) – and when it is so distinguished, the distinction is made in more than one way. According to some (*Anon. Seg.*

where the greatest scope for imaginative fiction was to be found.

An example of Libanius' technique will make the point. The 'misanthropist' or 'morose' old man (*dyskolos*)[7] has fallen over. His son simply laughed; and the father disinherits him. This is how he tells the tale:[8]

The other day, I was going down town from the farm. Not that I wanted to see anything here. Preserve me from thinking anything you've got worth troubling about! I'd damaged my mattock on the stones and needed it mending. That blacksmith – damn him! – only comes out to the farm on a fixed day, and collects a hefty fee for doing so; and this year he didn't come and so forced me to come down here. It was no pleasure to me to see him even there, and though I often had smith's work to be done, I said I hadn't, so as not to set eyes on him. However, seeing him here with a lot of other people was better than seeing him alone over there! Anyway, I was walking to find him, and I was upset, and cursing the wretched man all the time. This youngster here came with me uninvited; I didn't ask him to come – why should I? I didn't want his company. I often get angry with my own shadow because it always goes round with me, and that makes me cross with the sun and the moon, because they make the shadow. But somehow or other, when I was starting out, he kept out of my way and then appeared half-way through the journey. I was cross at first and nearly brought my stick down on him. I ought to have done so;

---

112 = p. 21 Graeven) it consists in 'establishing a position about matters which the jury know', whereas *diēgēsis* deals with facts they do not know. This does not correspond with Sopatros' usage; indeed *RG* VIII.3.9ff says the opposite. Closer to this is the definition in Apsines (251 Sp.–H.), which derives the *katastasis* from the speaker's own ideas and makes it 'remove objections' from the audience – in other words, it puts them in the appropriate state of mind. The word often means 'situation'; in this sense it is the term used in the Hippocratic *Epidemics* for the general climatic conditions which are the background to a particular outbreak of illness.

[7] Though Menander's *Dyskolos* is, in a sense, the basis of this and similar themes, it is important to emphasize that it is not Libanius' practice to paraphrase or copy closely any particular passage of comedy. There are surprisingly few verbal echoes of the *Dyskolos*, though the general setting is the same, and the same sort of ridiculous accident happens to the main character: in Menander, he falls down a well when he tries to retrieve his mattock. We may contrast the much closer use of Menander's play made by Aelian *Epistulae rusticae* 13–15.

[8] *Decl.* 27.3–8.

then he wouldn't have found me such a figure of fun. You can just imagine how he irritated me on the road, annoying the shepherds' dogs, throwing clods to scare away the cranes, chucking stones at the goats, or asking who someone was, or how much of the road was left. Anyone would think I had measured the roads or made a census of the population – I, who never meet anyone even accidentally, and never use the public road, but always go for my walk in the fields out of the way! But he thought I ought to know the people walking on the main road, and expected me to see sharper than an eagle!

Fed up as I was with all this, I stuck it out till we got to town and to the agora. The sight was intolerable. There were people laughing, swearing, abusing one another, carrying away food they never needed, each one of them a year's supply for a goodly number of persons capable of simple living. Not wanting to excite myself by looking at them, I withdrew my eyes so far as I could, and walked on not looking in front of my feet. I was not to know that I was myself the only person whom you force to obey the laws, or that you don't punish the controllers of the market and the police who despise them; they attend to municipal affairs so well that there are whole ponds in the city and slippery places all over the market. Into one of these I fell, not looking where I was going; my feet went from under me, and not being able to put my weight on my stick I fell down, and a proper laughing-stock I was for our young friend – though, ye gods! I never expected it. The moment I was on the ground, my mind turned to another thing; I was less frightened of the fall than that he or someone in the market would come and hold out their hand and ask me the usual questions – had I hurt my leg, broken my collar bone, crushed my hip? The vomit of words and questions would have killed me! But it didn't happen; quite unexpectedly, there was a splendid lack of humanity, as you would call it! But I could see *him*, with a happy look on his face, bursting with laughter and almost guffawing over me!

The features that make the *ēthos* are easily seen: the speaker hates company, pours scorn on the townsfolk's, and therefore the jury's, way of life, is equally dissatisfied whether the blacksmith comes or no, and comes to grief not by his own fault but because the Council has neglected to repair the pavement. This is obviously no exercise, but a comic entertainment.

3

The most famous of Libanius' declamations is the self-denunciation (*prosangelia*) of the *dyskolos* who finds life intolerable because of the talkativeness of his wife.[9] This was a favourite. It is highly praised in the forged correspondence of St Basil with Libanius, where it is said to have been a great success with 'the whole city'. Even women (we are told) listened to it; the author perhaps implies that they needed its lessons.

The character is displayed in the very first sentences. He 'ought to have died before marrying',[10] or at least as soon as possible thereafter; but as he has been so slow about making his suicide-application, he now hopes it will be dealt with expeditiously, lest his wife comes to court and spoils the pleasure of his death. The law, he insists, is meddlesome: it is 'slavery to make us ask for permission to put an end to our lives.' If the lawgiver hadn't been so fussy, I could just have taken a strap from my bed and hanged myself quietly on a tree in some lonely spot.'[11]

Serious litigants, of course, cannot criticize laws like this. Only an outrageous defendant in a declamation meant as entertainment dare do it. The trick occurs again: Libanius' miser complains of the expense demanded by the misguided lawgiver for weddings.[12]

The *katastasis* (5–23) begins with an account of the unfortunate speaker's upbringing. His father had always encouraged him to concentrate his mind, not to relax, and to hold fast to what is necessary in life. So he does not take part in politics – not, he hastens to add (for he needs the jurors' goodwill) because he is not interested in the common concerns of the city, but because he dislikes litigation, noise and the ridiculous habit of saying *khaire* ('Rejoice'), i.e., 'Good day', to people when there is nothing to

[9] *Decl.* 26; [Basil] *Epist.* 351 (in Foerster's Libanius, XI.591).
[10] Cf Sen. *Contr.* 6.6 with Winterbottom's note, p. 516. The problems of humourless or solitary men in marriage were a common comic theme: we recall Terence's Demea (*Adelphoe* 866) who complains: ego ille agrestis saevos tristis parcus truculentus tenax duxi uxorem: quam ibi miseriam vidi! nati filii: alia cura.
[11] Cf Menander, *Dyskolos* 169.   [12] *Decl.* 33.9.

rejoice about and it can do them no good.¹³ The truth is, he has an obsessive horror of noise: he avoids blacksmiths and silversmiths and all noisy places, and is shocked to find even painters (*zōgraphoi*) singing at their work.¹⁴

But he is unlucky enough to have Helpful Friends: a traditional motif, natural in comedy, and used elsewhere by Libanius.¹⁵ They advise him to marry. Indeed, they suggest a particular lady, who is very well off. He of course is interested only in one thing: 'What about her tongue?' He cannot bear snoring or hiccoughs or clearing the throat or coughing, let alone a chatterbox, even in a dream. His friend reassures him that silence has been the lady's special study, and she is as quiet as a statue. So the wedding takes place. It is of course an appallingly noisy affair, with much applause, laughter, unseemly dancing and an absurd wedding-song. It nearly made him throw away his garland and run out, but he endured it for the sake of the quiet night to come. But the wedding was peace compared with what was in store. Before midnight, the lady had broken silence: she complained of the bed, asked him if he was asleep, and just went on talking. In the morning he complained to the *nympheutria*¹⁶ (the bride's woman attendant who had arranged the marriage), only to be told that it was 'a sign of love', and 'a display of her voice'. But things get worse. The new mistress of the house interviews all the slave-women, asks their names and how many children they have had, and wants a complete inventory of the household effects. It turns out that there is no cock, because the master can't stand the crowing. To persuade him to get one, the wife plunges into a full-scale rhetorical encomium of the cock, 'how he was changed into a bird, and how he was a soldier, a servant of Ares, and all this is shown by his crest, his spurs and his fighting spirit'.¹⁷ Her husband leaves her at it, and complains to the

¹³ Cf *Decl.* 12.29.
¹⁴ Cf Horace, *Sat.* 2.5.90: difficilem et morosum (= δύσκολον) offendet garrulus; Sen. *Epist.* 56 on the philosopher's need to overcome his dislike of noise.
¹⁵ *Decl.* 33.
¹⁶ Here used, as the scholiast explains, for προμνήστρια ('matchmaker', as in Aristophanes, *Clouds* 41 etc.).
¹⁷ Cf [Liban.] *Progymnasmata, Narrationes* 26 (8.49 Foerster): 'The cock is a bird that was formerly a man. When he was a man, he was a bodyguard of Ares.

marriage-broker, who promises to do something about it. On his return, he faces (as always) a barrage of questions; if he is foolish enough to say anything, he fans the flame. He happens to mention that 'the general' has come home, and she seizes on this and goes hard at it from noon to evening: how many casualties were there, who were the officers commanding the tribes, who were the captains of the ships, how many men were there in the crews? 'Men's business', he replies: so she turns to country matters, and asks about the bushes and the mastic and the artichokes, or retails a lot of gossip about the market: the bakers are short of firewood; there's a scandal brewing about the silver-assayers. Worst of all is when she has been out herself. When she comes back from the bath, she gives her husband a regular shower of small talk.[18] She tells him who was there, and who was missing, who had servants with her and who had not, who has spots, who is getting wrinkled, who uses rouge, who brought soap, who lost her sandal, who upset the bathing-woman's wares, who gave the attendant an obol, and who gave him nothing and started a row... Momentarily at a loss, she 'cudgels herself' to recall something else; the husband lets a sigh escape him, and she at once seizes on this – there must be something wrong: is there anything out of place in the house? 'She lists the lot, down to the oil-flask and the soup-ladle.' 'Just be quiet', he says. 'Quiet! Why should I be quiet? Have I no rights?'[19] Off she goes on a catalogue of her ancestors, their provision of warships and tragic choruses – and *that* reminds her of tragedy, and she repeats the whole history of the genre from the very beginning. Even when the rest of her is asleep, her tongue is at its work – worse than the mosquitoes for keeping one awake!

Ares set him to watch the door of the bedroom, when he sinned against Hephaestus' bed, with orders to knock at the door before dawn, that he might not be caught in adultery. But both man and master slept, and the deed was known when morning came. So the soldier became a bird as a punishment. He bears many marks of the former soldier: his crest, his temper, his spurs. And, remembering the cause of his punishment, he drives sleep from men by his song before the Sun has yoked his chariot.'

[18] φεῦ τῆς ἐπομβρίας τῶν ῥημάτων. A classical metaphor: Thrasymachus (Pl. *Rep.* 1.344D) drenches his hearers 'like a bath-attendant' with his words.

[19] ἄτιμοι ('disfranchised persons') have no right of public speech.

The vast amount of domestic detail in all this is fascinating; much of it is from classical comedy — certainly many of the words are[20] — much also from works like Theophrastus' *Characters*,[21] but it is difficult not to concede Libanius a real sense of fun and a sharp eye for life.

Argument now follows; the speech, like most *prosangeliai*, comes under the *pragmatikē stasis*. The first point raised by the imagined opponent is that the normal conditions for an application of this kind have not been fulfilled. The applicant has neither lost his property nor been crippled nor suffered any misfortune of such magnitude as to make life intolerable. The answer to this is indignant: 'Are you my father? Or my brother or my uncle? My cousin perhaps? A business or farming partner?' If one wants to die, it is one's own business; the shame of it is that it takes so many words to argue the case! 'You ask why I want to die. Because of *you*.[22] Am I not right, members of Council, to be distraught and out of my wits? I expected to find the Council House more merciful than home, and I find the people here worse than what I have left!' The rhetors, always on the make, naturally think loss of property the worst thing that can happen; but it is not irreversible, many have made a second fortune. The speaker's troubles, he claims, are of the mind,[23] and are inconsolable; no future pleasure can counteract them, for they

---

[20] E.g. (a few instances only): λύζω (10) ~ Aristophanes, *Acharn.* 690; θαλαττοκοπεῖ (18) ~ *Knights* 830; σπαθᾶν (32) ~ *Clouds* 55; βρωμώμενοι (36) ~ *Wasps* 618; κινεῖν τὸν ἀνάγυρον (21) ~ *Lysistrata* 68; ἡμιτύβιον (42) ~ *Plutus* 729.

[21] See esp. Theophrastus' Garrulous Man (ἀδολέσχης), Talkative Man (λάλος)

[22] At p. 529, 1 Foerster follows Gasda in adding ⟨οὐ⟩; I believe this to be wrong.

[23] 29: σῶόν ἐστί μοι τὸ σῶμα, τὴν δὲ ψυχήν, ὦ φίλτατοι, βέβλαμμαι. μεστός εἰμι ῥημάτων ἀνοήτων. μήκεσιν ἀπείροις λόγων βέβλημαι. ἀδολεσχίαις βεβάπτισμαι. πολλὴν δέδεγμαι γλωσσαλγίαν. καθάπερ πλοῖον θάλαττα, ὑπερέσχε με τῆς γυναικὸς ὁ κλύδων. οὐκ εἰμὶ φρενήρης. ἰλιγγιῶ, σκοτοδινιῶ. ('My body is safe, but, friends, I am hurt in the mind. I am burdened with foolish words. I am struck down by infinitely long speeches. I am deluged with chatter. I am at the receiving end of a terrible tongue-ache. The wife's wave swamps me as the sea swamps a boat. I am not in my right mind. I am dazzled, I am dizzy.') This is deliberately written in short phrases (κομματικῶς) to vary the periodic manner of most of the speech (cf below, n. 41).

make all the favours of fortune vain. Besides, we all have different fears: to some poverty is the worst of ills, to some loss of children, exile or sickness; to the speaker, it is talk. He could have put up with a drunken wife – she would have dozed off sometimes – or a silly one, or an extravagant one, but not with this. Every encounter with her brings him near death; is it not better to die once for all? She is an 'Arab piper',[24] she chatters more than a dove or a daw or a nightingale or a monkey. The gongs of Dodona are silent when the wind drops; not so she.[25] He prayed – he tells us – for deafness; but the gods would not grant it. There is noise everywhere: in the market, in the country – frogs, donkeys and cows, sheep and goats – and even in court; 'the rhetors are worse than the frogs'. Home should be the only refuge, and this is denied. Even when his wife is ill, it never seems to affect her voice – she never gets pharyngitis or a tongue ulcer or inflamed tonsils, whatever else befalls her.

The vigorous detail, the learned language, and a certain incoherence and repetition make this part, like the *katastasis*, a display of humour and character rather than of persuasive argument. Two other *antitheseis* make up the rest of the speech:

(i) 'You brought it on yourself, because you failed to educate her.'[26] Answer: 'I tried, but it was to no avail.' Indeed, his efforts went against him. He brought in friends who had prepared 'encomia of silence', but she was a match for them all. He quoted Sophocles' 'Silence brings adornment unto women'. She at once asked who wrote the line, who was his father, what was his deme, when he commenced poet, and how he died. And when the husband talked about cicadas, among whom the males chatter and the females are silent,[27] she countered by telling the whole myth.

---

[24] Cf *Epist.* 758, Zenobius 2.39 etc.: proverbial, the idea being that the Arabs took turns piping in the watches of the night, keeping the fire burning till morning. Knowledge of this probably comes from comedy or commentary on comedy, cf Menander, *Anatithemene*, fr. 30 Koerte, Cantharus fr. 1 Kock.

[25] Cf Menander fr. 66 Kock.

[26] §38.

[27] Cf Aristotle, *HA* 5.30, Aelian, *NA* 11.26. Here is a display of a different, but also very popular, form of *historia*, viz. vulgarized natural history, akin to 'paradoxography'.

Even gagging her was useless, for she screamed the house down as soon as the gag was removed.

(ii) 'Why do you not put her away?'[28] There are two answers to this. First, she would herself have to come to court, with what consequences one can easily guess. The odd thing about this argument is the legal background. It appears that in Attic law,[29] the husband could dismiss the wife without any legal process. Here, Libanius implies (as usual) that the Council deals with *prosangeliai* and it is not the law for the wife to be present at this hearing; but if it was a jury-court, and the case concerned her expulsion from the matrimonial home, he tells us that she would have equal access to the court with her husband. Secondly, he would have had to suffer the ridicule of her friends and family, to be called a humourless eccentric, and to endure continual expostulations from her relatives, while she herself laid siege to the house and filled the neighbourhood with her screaming.

The epilogue is an appeal for eternal rest; he wants to be allowed to drink the hemlock in peace, without his wife being present: 'Sweet it is to enjoy the daylight and take pleasure, but my wife deprives me of this.'[30] One would think this to be the end of the matter; but the speaker goes on a little. It is not only what she does but what she will do that drives him to death. Suppose she produces a litter of offspring like herself: 'My house will be like a meadow where flocks of birds cry and fly around'.[31]

He has strayed from the line of his argument. He has caught talkativeness from his wife. But he finally comes to a halt: 'O happy day, O day of freedom! I go to those below, to those who do not talk. I shall find a place full of quiet.'

4

The miser, like the misanthropist, is a favourite character of comedy and of popular philosophy. In Libanius, for example, he 'denounces himself' when he has become entangled with a prostitute who wants money,[32] or when he finds buried treasure

---

[28] §44.
[29] Harrison (1968) 40.
[30] §62.
[31] The allusion is to *Iliad* 2.459.
[32] Liban. *Decl.* 32, cf *RG* VIII.309.

which proves to be less in value than the tax to be paid for its discovery.[33] In another declamation of the same school, he disowns a son who has vowed a talent to Asclepius for his father's recovery from illness.[34] In the case I discuss now,[35] the miser's son is an *aristeus*, and makes a foolish choice of reward: a crown of wild olive. The father seeks to 'disown' him.

The speech, though somewhat more elaborate than that of the *dyskolos*, is still very simply constructed. Like all 'reward disputes', it would be counted by many teachers as an example of the *pragmatikē stasis*. But it is also possible to treat it as *antilēpsis*, in the sense that the boy's legitimate choice is taken by the father as something which requires defence. The basic structure is again: prologue (1–5); *katastasis* (6–27); no less than six objections (*antitheseis*) with their refutations (28–47); and an epilogue (48–55) which includes an epideictic 'encomium of wealth'. It is in the choice of *antitheseis* that the resemblance of the case to *antilēpsis* becomes apparent.

Once again, the *ēthos* of the speaker is established at the outset. The old man begins by saying that he cannot find fault with his son for doing so well in the war,[36] because he has saved 'both property and lives' – in that order. But the boy's foolishness in the matter of the reward cancels it all out. He is 'wiser than his father'; the two cannot possibly live together, and the boy must leave home. The jury will understand how dreadful it is to be deprived of a gain on which you counted; are they not looking forward to their fee?

This is an ingenious opening. It displays the issue as one between the lover of wealth and the lover of honour, so that the paradoxical and ironical tone of the whole becomes apparent, for it is only in irony that one can so obviously take the wrong side in the moral conflict. Also, it sets the piece in the world of Aristophanes. Here are the greedy jurymen of the *Wasps*, the disenchanted father of the *Clouds*.

[33] Liban. *Decl.* 31, cf *RG* VIII.315. [34] [Liban.] *Decl.* 34.
[35] Liban. *Decl.* 33: φιλαργύρου παῖς ἀριστεύσας ᾔτησεν εἰς τὴν δωρεὰν θαλλοῦ στέφανον καὶ ἀποκηρύσσεται.
[36] As the scholiast points out, this is to counter the prejudice of the jury, who will have assumed that the father disapproved of his son's ἀριστεία.

The *katastasis* – ingeniously introduced by an apostrophe to the son[37] – begins with the marriage. Long postponed because of the expense involved, it was finally undertaken on the advice of Helpful Friends. They had reminded the miser that he would be old one day, and in need of support, and had suggested that he might have a son who was commercially minded (*emporikos*) and might even be a better manager than his father. Such promises were visionary; but the friends had a more substantial and present argument. The lady they were putting forward was rich. Yet, however delightful the future advantages, the immediate expense is painful. 'Who can be the lawgiver who made us spend so much on wine and perfume and torches?' 'Won't the bridegroom know what to do unless there are a lot of people standing round the door?' Here again is the ironical criticism of the lawgiver, the rude divergence from the usual courtesies which is in character for the miser, as for the misanthropist, and which reveals the speech as a parody.

In fact, the wife turned out well. She worked hard, ate little, and bathed only at the new moon.[38] But her son, who might have been expected to fall naturally into his father's ways, proved very different. He had no interest in money. The advice of the friends was therefore sought. What career was suitable for him? Should he become a philosopher? An economical life, of course – long hair and not many baths; but the contempt for money advocated by the moralists more than outweighed the advantages. An athlete? The father reacts strongly against this suggestion: 'What is he to bring me back from Olympia? A crown of wild olive? A worthy return for the oil and the fees one will have to pay his trainer!' This premonition of the dreadful future is passed over quickly. The miser decides to make his son

[37] 6: οὐκ ἐπὶ ταύταις, ὦ παῖ, ταῖς προσδοκίαις οὔτε τὴν μητέρα σου ἠγόμην οὔτε σὲ ἐποιούμην. μᾶλλον δέ, τί μοι πρὸς τουτονὶ τὸν ἀπόπληκτον ἀλλ' οὐ πρὸς ὑμᾶς περὶ τῶν ἐμαυτοῦ διαλεκτέον; ('These were not the expectations, my son, with which I married your mother and begot you. But why am I discussing my affairs with this lunatic and not with you, the jury?'). The apostrophe to the son strongly resembles a common feature in funeral speeches: cf, e.g. Menander Rhetor 435.3ff.

[38] Frequent baths are a known sign of luxury: Sen. *Epist.* 86.

a farmer; this is a profession in which rewards are sure, for even in bad weather there are profitable sidelines — selling hurdles and firewood.[39] The soliloquy in which this is said, and the following 'advice' to the son over dinner are good examples of *ēthopoiia*. Much of the material would be familiar to young students; the 'encomium of farming' was a common elementary exercise.[40] And the style shows a good deal of variety, diverging widely from the periodic manner of the main argument: 'You are strong. You can work. We've a farm. You see my way. Don't be afraid to imitate. Bear a lot of injury rather than lose a drachma. A little medicine cures wounds, the money's gone for good.'[41] Needless to say, the boy will have nothing of this. He chooses instead to become a soldier. More expense: instruction in tactics, purchase of shields and spears, a gilded shield-boss and a crest for his helmet. And the exercise produces an enormous appetite. The father is on the point of disowning his son because he cannot afford to keep him.

At this point, the well-intentioned friends reappear — just as, in the *dyskolos* declamation, they try to patch up the marriage they originally advocated. They urge that it would not be a bad thing to have a soldier son. Many soldiers wear gold in battle; the man who kills them takes it, and the general is none the wiser. And only suppose the young man were to win the prize for bravery!

The old man is convinced, and makes another little speech to his son: 'Go on, then, steal the bracelets and necklaces off the bodies in the camp, and make sure no one knows about it. Rush out in front of the main body; either you'll die (we all come to that) or you'll make me very rich.' The victory is won, and the father is in a state of great excitement and thoughtless extravagance. A second lamp is lit, the proportion of water in the wine is reduced, and he goes so far as to sacrifice a laying hen, despite

[39] Cf Virgil, *Georgics* 1.259ff.
[40] Encomium of farming: Libanius VIII.261ff Foerster.
[41] 16: ἔρρωταί σοι τὸ σῶμα. δύνασαι πονεῖν. ἔστιν ἡμῖν χωρίον. ὁρᾷς τὴν ἐμὴν ὁδόν. μὴ γένῃ κακὸς εἰς τὸν ζῆλον. μᾶλλον ὑπόμεινον πλῆθος τραυμάτων ἢ δραχμῆς ἀποστῆναι. τὰ μὲν γὰρ ἴασιν δέχεται μικρῷ φαρμάκῳ, τὰ δὲ οἴχεται. Cf above n. 23.

the loss of her eggs.⁴² So the returning warrior dines well; he tells his father the whole story of the battle, but refuses to reveal what reward he will choose, merely putting on a solemn air and saying it will be a very great thing. It is an unpromising sign that he wastes the wine on a libation to Ares. The father goes to bed in suspense, and tosses all night, complaining of the length of the night (like Strepsiades at the beginning of the *Clouds*) and sending his servant out repeatedly to see if it is morning. At last the happy day dawns. Friends arrive to escort father and son to the Assembly. The young man mounts the platform. He rubs his head – like Demosthenes in Aeschines' hostile narrative⁴³ – looks round and tells the story of the battle at length. This prolongs the suspense, and also detracts from the sympathetic *ēthos* of the young man; the *dēmos* (if we may believe the father) becomes restive at his boasting. But at last he names his request, the valueless wreath.⁴⁴ The decree is passed. The father has to be restrained by force from tearing his son's eyes out, and makes his way home in a daze – he 'hardly recognizes the street' – and dismays his wife by his air of despondency.

This delicate and humorous narrative – Lucianic in tone, but arguably superior to Lucian – is followed by a sudden change of tone. The speaker has just reported his conversation with his wife. 'My dear', she says, 'has the reward made you like this?' 'Yes', he replies, 'it *was* like this.' The flat despair is succeeded by the indignation with which he now states his complaint: 'I have suffered the most dreadful wrong, members of the jury'. This *probolē* introduces the objections and their answers, which form the argumentative structure of the speech. The boy's defence is imagined as made up of seven points:

⁴² Cf Aristophanes, *Clouds* 663.
⁴³ τρίψας τὴν κεφαλήν, Aeschines, *Fals. leg.* 49. LSJ say it signifies 'perplexity' (as 'rubbing your head' does with us), but V. Martin (Budé ed., ad loc.) calls it 'une inconvenance', and refers to Aeschines, *C. Timarch.* 25, where Aeschines expresses a dislike of extravagant gesture. One might also connect it with the Latin *frontem fricare*, which commonly connotes shamelessness, and this would suit here; but note also that *frontem ferire*, Cic. *Att.* 1.1, is a sign of dismay and incomprehension.
⁴⁴ 'A shadow of smoke', καπνοῦ σκιάν. Libanius uses a proverbial expression: Soph. *Antigone* 1170, Macarius 5.4.

(i) The law of *apokēryxis* does not apply to *aristeis* ('demurrer', *paragraphikon*);[45]
(ii) he has not done anything deserving *apokēryxis*, like squandering his father's property in gambling or lavish dinners[46] (*paragraphikon horikon*);
(iii) his request was perfectly legal (*antilēpsis*);
(iv) honour is more important than wealth;
(v) and (vi) he badly wanted a crown, and one given by decree ('forgiveness', *syngnōmē*);
(vii) he hates money (frame of mind, *gnōmē*).

The refutation of (i) is a clear parody. The miser accuses the boy of being a 'clever sophist' when he wishes to injure his parent, but a silly baby[47] in matters of money: he has neglected the simple duty to choose the cash. And unless he can point to a clause which specifically exempts *aristeis* from being disowned, he cannot claim the support of the law ('lawgiver's intention'). The second point (ii) is answered by saying that he has done something just as bad, namely frustrated his father's hopes (*anthorismos, pēlikotēs, pros ti*). This is supported by four *exempla*:[48] the boy is like a slave who brings home only half the earnings he could; he is like a vine that bears no fruit; he is the general who fails to fulfil his promises, or the dream that deceives. 'All disappointment of expectations is damage.' In fact, the father was so clearly convinced that he was going to be rich that he actually took the clothes out of the clothes-chest and prepared it to receive the expected gold. He is very distressed indeed; he points to his emaciated appearance and the feebleness of his voice. Worst of all, he has to endure the ridicule of neighbours and slave-girls.

[45] Cf *RG* VIII.131ff.
[46] With §31, compare Aeschines, *C. Timarch.* 95.
[47] ἠλίθιος, ἀγροῖκος, κορύζης καὶ λέμφου ἔμπλεως ('babyish, boorish, full of mucus and catarrh'). These words are from comedy, gleaned no doubt from Atticist lexica: cf Moeris 251 Pierson: λέμφος ἡ πεπηγυῖα μύξα 'Ἀττικῶς, Ammonius, *De adfinium vocabulorum differentia* 296 Nickau: λέμφοι δὲ παρὰ 'Ἀττικοῖς οἱ κορυζώδεις ἐλέγοντο καὶ μυξώδεις. Μένανδρος Ὑποβολιμαίῳ (fr. 427 Koerte²) γέρων †ἀμέμικτ'† ἄθλιος λέμφος.
[48] Strictly *parabolai*, which were distinguished from *paradeigmata* (historical examples) as being drawn from life in general and not from specific events or persons (Minucianus, *RG* IX.604).

Objection (iii) is answered by saying that it is also legal for the father to throw his son out. Fathers have total control over their children; the jury must see this, and not allow a dangerous precedent which would subvert their own households. Everything the boy has ever eaten or drunk or worn is the father's, his equipment likewise. This is clearly a display of *ēthos*; and so is everything that follows. To prefer honour to wealth (iv) is, the father declares, the teaching of vain quacks – he means philosophers – who are near starving themselves. 'Honour' can neither be seen nor touched, it fills no purse, it buys no commodities. As to the boy's passion for a garland (v), he could have ten, taken off the olive-trees – or roses, for that matter, if he had wanted something more expensive.[49] No need to bring the people to a meeting for that; but having done so – if the honorific decree really was an essential part of his ambition (vi) – he might at least have asked for a crown of gold. Finally (vii), if money is so objectionable, why not ask for free meals for himself and his father,[50] since the family is clearly going to be ruined by his folly?

The epilogue is an ingenious display of rhetorical virtuosity. It returns to the theme of the opening paragraphs, the incompatibility of father and son. But it develops into an encomium of wealth – pure *thesis* material, a *progymnasma* embedded in a *meletē* – and it ends with a *sententia* which Seneca might have admired: '"How am I to live?", the boy may say. "Win the prize again, and ask for gold!"'[51]

5

A variant of this theme is the subject of two declamations of Choricius, 'The Young Hero' and 'The Miser'.[52] In these, the father has arranged a wealthy marriage for his son; but the young man, returning victorious from the wars, asks as his reward to

---

[49] A similar sentiment in a philosophical context is Epictetus 1.19.29: εἰ ἅπαξ ἐπιθυμεῖς στεφάνου, ῥοδινὸν λαβὼν περίθου ('if you just want a garland, get one of roses and put it on').

[50] σίτησις ἐν πρυτανείῳ for which Socrates so impudently asked (Pl. *Apol.* 37A).

[51] §55: ἀριστεύσας πάλιν, αἴτησον χρυσίον.

[52] Choricius, *Decl.* 5 and 6.

be allowed to marry a beautiful but poor girl with whom he has fallen in love at a festival, and whom his father has hitherto refused to consider. In Libanius' speech, as we have seen, the conflict was between love of honour and love of money, and the humour lay in imagining how the case for money could be put, however contrary it is to common sympathy. In Choricius, the battle is between love of money and romantic love.

Choricius' introductory explanation[53] is illuminating. He begins by explaining that 'the laws of the art admit children disputing with parents, because *plasmata* reproduce all the cases that occur in experience'. This sounds defensive; perhaps in the Christian culture of sixth-century Syria, there was a particular need to justify the use of themes which might be thought subversive of parental authority. In this case,

> the young man has many means at his disposal to attract the people to his cause. He has routed an enemy attack, and rescued his country from danger. He has the law on his side, and asks a reasonable reward in the form of a girl brought up in poverty.

That is to say, at first sight the case seems very one-sided. But

> despite this abundance of justification, he is not without anxiety, nor is he confident of winning the case so painlessly. The issue is between child and father, poverty and wealth — and wealth is dear to all men, and especially valued by the miser. He will thus combine a certain degree of youthful arrogance with a certain amount of flattery, taking pride in his war-service, but showing himself humble before his father even after his victory, lest some of the audience judge his whole life-style by the present dispute, suspect him of being quarrelsome and impudent toward his parents, and so lend him a less friendly ear.

> Of course it would have been best for the boy to have risen superior to love; but since he failed in this, the next best course is for him to try not to be thought dissolute, by making the point that this is his first love affair, and that he did not take the girl by violence or indulge in any of the disgraceful acts to which lovers are often impelled. He thus frees himself from the imputation of disorderly conduct and does greater honour to his girl by showing how her beauty has prevailed even over so chaste a young man. As well as taking this line, he will

[53] *Or.* 26 (= *Decl.* 5), *theōria*, p. 225 F.–R. Cf above, ch. 4, p. 83.

also try as far as possible to make her appear convincingly preferable to the rich young lady; and if he sometimes seems to go too far in his praise of her, this is to be condoned in a lover.

It is easy to see how this plan is carried out in the actual speech.

(i) The girl's beauty is emphasized right at the start. Indeed – the young man says – had it been proper for her to appear in the assembly, her appearance would have won the day without the need for words.

(ii) At the same time, the boy repeatedly stresses his deference to his father. He tells us that his friends used to make fun of him for being so tied to his father, like a slave;[54] and it is with the greatest hesitation that he brought himself (he says) to open the question of the girl. He and his father had been together to the festival at which he had seen her; on the way home, the father discoursed on the extravagance of such occasions, while the son (who was thinking of one girl only) talked generally about the charm and good manners of the ladies they had seen. It was not till some time later that he ventured to approach the real question; he prepared a convincing speech, and found what he thought to be a favourable moment. But he got no further than expounding the proposition that a man of means ought, in general, to consider beauty rather than wealth in selecting a wife, when the look on his father's face made it clear that it was useless to go on.

(iii) So he tries to forget the girl. But he cannot. To explain his feelings, he uses an image which Choricius has chosen to remind us that this is a brave man talking, someone who knows what fear and courage are:[55]

Just as a man who suffers from the sickness of cowardice, and naturally becomes very frightened as he walks in a lonely place in the dark, makes matters worse if he tries to put his fear out of his mind, so I found myself inadvertently kindling the flame by the very means by which I was trying to put it out.

(iv) The speaker states, as is usual, a number of imaginary objections which he then proceeds to answer. One of these is the

[54] §6. Contrast the argument of Libanius' miser that parents have total ownership of their children and all that is theirs (above, p. 101).   [55] §48.

suggestion that he fought in the war in order to win the girl, not out of patriotism. But he does not attribute this outrageous suggestion to his father, but to an unknown citizen who 'no doubt was not here when the war broke out'.[56] Once again, the father's decency is preserved.

(v) And so it is in the epilogue. The young man promises to teach his wife to honour his father. And indeed he feels convinced that his father will soon relent:

He is already giving me a gentle, paternal look; his expression is that of a man who is giving way. He did not come here intending to harm me, but merely to demonstrate to you that I am not a man led to say rash things even when we are quarrelling; he often tests me like this, by pretending to oppose me.[57]

The art of disarming could scarcely go further, and that is what *ēthos* is all about.

[56] §58. [57] §74.

6
Declamation and history

> Concessum est rhetoribus ementiri in historiis ut aliquid dicere possint argutius.
>
> 'Rhetors are allowed to tell lies in their history, so as to be in a position to say something more pointed.'
>
> Cicero

I

We saw that the imaginary themes (*plasmata*) of the declaimers are set vaguely in the classical past. Sometimes the mere addition of names turns them into a sort of rudimentary historical fiction. Often, however, the effort of historical imagination is more profound. There is here a distinct difference between Latin practice and Greek. In the Latin schools, historical pieces were usually *suasoriae*, and so thought easier and less important than the forensic *controversiae*;[1] but at the same time there seems to have been a greater readiness to adopt themes of contemporary or recent history.[2] In Greek, historical themes are used both for deliberative and for forensic exercises, but they are almost entirely confined to the classical past.

The use of such themes goes back to the beginnings of rhetoric. Gorgias' *Helen* and *Palamedes* are relevant, for the difference

---

[1] Tacitus, *Dialogus* 35.4, Quint. 2.1.3.

[2] Kohl (1915) lists 73 Roman themes (nos. 357–429). The Punic Wars naturally suggested many subjects. The first-century B.C. text-books (*Ad Herennium*, *De inventione*) propose topics from comparatively recent history (Popilius and the Gauls, trial of Caepio, parricide of Malleolus [101 B.C.], Saturninus, the Social War); this is probably an adaptation of Greek practice to the newly established Roman schools. The unpopularity of the rhetors with the Roman government (Suet. *Rhet.* 1) may be connected with the political tone of these exercises. Later, Seneca has little Roman history, only a few themes about Cicero; the civil war was naturally a source of material in imperial times.

Declamation and history

between the mythical and the historical past is not significant.[3] One of the earliest pieces of evidence we have — a Berlin papyrus of the third century B.C.[4] — is an imaginary defence of the four 'advocates' attacked in the last part of Demosthenes' speech against Leptines; similar topics were in use in the schools of the Empire too, for Aristides, Apsines and Lollianus all used the Leptines story.[5]

In all, we know of about 350 themes of Greek history treated by the declaimers. A few are mythological, 43 deal with the Persian war, about 90 with the Peloponnesian war, 125 with the period of Demosthenes, and 25 or so with Alexander. There is hardly anything later. Himerius' declamation on Epicurus accused of impiety[6] and the similar one known to Syrianus in which Epicurus is examined as to his suitability for the office of torch-bearer in the Mysteries[7] are thinly disguised philosophical theses, and perhaps owe their popularity to the closer links between philosophy and rhetoric in the fourth and fifth centuries of our era. It is surprising that there is not more use of Hellenistic themes; the reason may be that the 'classicizing' movement of the early Empire not only purged the style of rhetoric of many Hellenistic features, but also dismissed Hellenistic subjects. A surviving exception is recorded by Seneca: Greek rhetors apparently used the story of Flamininus executing a criminal in order to gratify the whim of a prostitute — a sharply anti-Roman anecdote.[8]

This concentration on the classical period is clearly important. It reminds us that one of the major purposes of the whole educational process of which *meletē* formed a part was the preservation of a sense of pride in the Hellenic inheritance, a sort

---

[3] *Historia* covers both real history and myth. In later times, at least, mythical themes were common in declamation: there are Trojan war subjects in Aristides, Libanius and Choricius.

[4] *P. Berol.* 9781, ed. K. Kunst (Berl. Klassikertexte VII, 1923).

[5] Aristides, *Or.* 47D (= *Or.* 4) 3 (see Boulanger [1923] 275); *Or.* 53–4 are Byzantine work (by Thomas Magister). See also Apsines 252.16 Sp.–H.; and (for Lollianus) Philostratus, *VS* 527.   [6] Himerius, *Or.* 3 Colonna.

[7] *RG* IV.719.   [8] *Contr.* 9.2.25, cf Livy 39.43.

of Hellenic patriotism, distinct from, but not necessarily in conflict with, loyalty to the institutions of imperial Rome. The rhetors seem to have lived largely in the past, in a world whose glitter made the present relatively unimportant and insignificant. It is natural to ask whether this was really so, whether sometimes these remote themes were used as a cover for comment on the contemporary scene. Mythological poetry was apparently so used: Maternus in Tacitus' *Dialogus* professes to use tragedy without fear of offence to indicate an attitude to current events: *si qua omisit Cato, sequenti recitatione Thyestes dicet*.[9]

Did Greek declamation ever serve a similar need? The possible examples are few and uncertain. (i) Lollianus,[10] who was *stratēgos* at Athens, involved his pupils in contributing to pay for a cargo of grain from Thessaly, in a time of shortage; he also composed a denunciation of Leptines based on the failure of the corn-supply from Pontus. But it is not stated that he used the declamation in support of his political initiative. (ii) A case in Sopatros[11] suggests what must have been a common situation in the time of the barbarian invasions: a force of mercenaries is granted land to settle in lieu of wages; they build a city; their employers subsequently want to buy them out, but in vain. (iii) Libanius' 'Defence of Socrates' has been thought to be related to Julian's anti-Christian policies.[12] The date fits (later than January 362), and it is true that Socrates served as a symbol whom the pagan philosophers could oppose to Christ. But the elaborate speech gives no convincing hint, unless the composition of so large-scale a work – well outside the ordinary proportions of a declamation – is itself evidence of an ulterior purpose.

In default of clearer evidence, we should be sceptical. But

---

[9] *Dialogus* 3. This is of course Latin evidence, not Greek; and the Romans (see above, n. 2) were more inclined to make teaching 'relevant' to their own public life.

[10] Philostratus, *VS* 526–7; cf *RG* VIII.316 for another case involving the food supply of a city.

[11] *RG* VIII.325. Dr Winterbottom reminds me of the parallel of the Saxons in Britain (Gildas, *De excidio* 23–4).

[12] Bowersock (1978) 19 n. 26; cf Libanius, *Epist.* 362, and Markowski (1910) 169f.

declaimers had at least the opportunity to allude to their own times; tyrant themes and 'rich man' themes could easily be exploited as comment and propaganda. Perhaps they were, though the circumstances – often local and ephemeral – escape us.

In general, the concentration on the past must have been escapism. In some writers – as in Aristides – it produced a real imaginative grasp of the classical world; in others, it was shallow and trivial, no better than the superficiality of a bad historical novel or film.

2

The stylistic side of it all is clearly important. There was a close link between imaginative expertise and the carefully fostered linguistic skill of reproducing classical Attic. This is a familiar feature of all the literature of the Empire; but the particular way in which this linguistic *mimēsis* was practised by the declaimers needs to be defined. While Atticizing historians like Arrian modelled themselves often on specific *exempla* – Xenophon, for example – the declaimers, or at least the mass of them, were not in the business of reproducing specific pastiches of Demosthenes or Lysias. They had their own styles and manners, schools and rivalries. Some indulged more in point and conceit, others aimed at a more sober manner. They were of course steeped in what they called *ta biblia*[13] – 'the books', the corpus of classical writing that could almost be called their 'bible' – and they took pains over the pedigree of the rarer words they used. Some had favourite classical authors, perhaps rather obscure, whom they took pride in reviving; Herodes[14] reintroduces a taste for the sophist Critias, despite his reputation as an anti-democrat; Proclus of Naucratis[15] has a touch of Hippias and Gorgias in his manner. But their choice of vocabulary was not confined to the orators, or even to the orators and historians together; rare words from comedy have an honoured place.[16] It is, I think, significant that

---

[13] τὰ βιβλία: [Dion. Hal.] *Ars* 298 U.–R. The term is used of the biblical corpus from the time of Origen.
[14] Philostratus, *VS* 564.   [15] Ibid. 604.
[16] Cf ch. 5, n. 20, n. 47 for examples from Libanius.

they did not, in general, feel any obligation to change their tune in accordance with the particular orator whose part they were momentarily playing. Hyperides was a favourite figure in their fictions. He proposes a bodyguard for Demosthenes after Elatea; he moves the enfranchisement of disenfranchised rhetors after Chaeronea; he defends Demosthenes against Philip's demand for his surrender.[17] Now Hyperides was famous for elegance and delicacy. He was a true model of Attic urbanity; 'no one', as ps.-Longinus says, 'feels frightened when he reads him.'[18] Yet the declamatory reproductions of Hyperides[19] make no attempt at these qualities. Himerius indeed seems consciously to aim not at this but at grandeur and force.[20] The rhetorical needs of the situation are more important than fidelity to the known style of the orator who is to be impersonated.

There is an apparent exception to this in the pair of speeches composed by Libanius for Menelaus and Odysseus on their mission to the Trojans asking for the return of Helen.[21] These are of course based on the belief that Homer's descriptions of the oratory of Menelaus and Odysseus figure the main varieties of style.[22] Menelaus speaks 'few words but clear'; Odysseus' eloquence is 'like winter snows'. Menelaus is therefore designedly concise and restrained, Odysseus forceful and periodic – and twice as long-winded. But even as a demonstration of two ideal styles, this pair of speeches is not at all clearly differentiated. Libanius seems, even here, to have been content to give a very general impression.

[17] Apsines 217, 234 Sp.–H.; Himerius, *Or.* 1.
[18] [Longin.] *De sublimitate* 34.4.
[19] Himerius loc. cit., [Liban.] *Decl.* 18.
[20] See p. 13.5 Colonna: οὐδὲ τοῖς γυμνοῖς χρῆσθαι τῶν ὀνομάτων, ἀλλὰ τοῖς δι' ἐμφάσεως τὸ βούλημα σημαίνουσιν ('and not using bare words but those which signify intention by innuendo'), with Longin. *Rhet.* 216 Sp.–H.: ὅτι ἐπὶ δεινῷ λόγῳ οὐ χρὴ τοῖς γυμνοῖς χρῆσθαι τῶν ὀνομάτων ἀλλὰ τοῖς δι' ἐμφάσεως τὸ βούλημα σημαίνουσιν ('in forcible writing one should not use bare words but those which signify intention by innuendo'). So *emphasis* ('innuendo') is characteristic of 'forcefulness', and Himerius (if indeed he, and not a later commentator, wrote the first passage quoted) intends his speech as 'forcible' (*deinos*).
[21] Liban. *Decl.* 3–4.
[22] Radermacher (1951) 6–9: Russell, '*Longinus*' *On the Sublime* (Oxford 1964), Intr., xxxvi n. 3.

3

Despite this lack of individualized *mimēsis*, the rhetorical schools were always capable of producing speeches which could pass as genuine classical works. Indeed, some of their efforts have done so even in modern times. It is one of the curiosities of scholarship that serious historians have taken the *Peri Politeias* ascribed to Herodes Atticus as a work of the late fifth century B.C.[23] This little speech, which is a deliberative piece spoken by a Thessalian in favour of alliance with Sparta against Archelaos of Macedon, bears the familiar marks of deliberative declamation: the argument moves under the heads of 'necessity' and 'expediency', and several imagined objections are stated and answered. Tradition assigns it to Herodes; though the accounts of Herodes' style do not support this, we must remember that the accounts of Polemon's 'torrential' style seem equally inappropriate to the extant texts attributed to him;[24] the argument against Herodes on this score is therefore not strong. Knowledge of Thessalian affairs is conspicuous; if Herodes is not the author, one might think of Hippodromos of Larissa.

Confusion between declamations and genuine speeches existed even in antiquity. Dionysius of Halicarnassus knew that there were speeches in the corpus of the Attic orators which were 'foolish and sophistical': the speech of Dinarchus on not surrendering Harpalus to Alexander was an example.[25] Speeches of Pericles were in circulation, but widely known to be false, for he left no written work behind.[26] Most striking of all, there is the surviving speech of Demades, 'On the Twelve Years', preserved in the manuscript tradition of the Attic Orators, but rightly regarded as one of the numerous declamatory exercises in which Demades is a speaker.[27] Of course, speeches could be

---

[23] Review of opinions in the edition by U. Albini (Florence 1968). The best-known advocate of a fifth-century date is the historian H. T. Wade-Gery (*CQ* XXXIX [1945] 19–33).
[24] See above, ch. 4, n. 36.
[25] Dion. Hal. *Dinarchus* 11.
[26] Plutarch, *Pericles* 8; Quint. 12.2.22; Meinhardt (1957) 86ff.
[27] Ed. V. de Falco, *Demade oratore* (Naples 1954).

forged for other reasons than for the purposes of the schools; but that a certain number of declamations came to be taken for the genuine article seems certain.

4

We should not forget another context in which speeches resembling historical *meletai* had long been composed, namely in history itself. The practice antedates the beginnings of rhetorical teaching, for which it often provided a model. It is no wonder that the declaimers studied Thucydides minutely and were much influenced by his style and manner of thinking. This is particularly clear in Aristides, and especially in the 'Sicilian' speeches.[28] But it is clear also in Sopatros,[29] when he presents the case for and against the Corinthians accused of damage to the Greek nation because of the long and distressing war which resulted from their complaints; 'The organization and division of the case', he says, 'is to be found in Archidamus' speech and that of the Corinthians.'[30] But it would of course be both provocative and misleading to call Thucydides the first declaimer. True, when he says he is putting *ta deonta* ('what was needed') into the mouths of his speakers,[31] he professes no more than any declaimer might profess; and the precise nature of the commitment to truth which he makes in claiming to keep 'as close as possible' to the 'overall intention' (*xympasa gnōmē*) remains uncertain. But there is an essential difference between historian and rhetor. The historian subordinates his speeches to the general view of the situation as he understands it. If, like Thucydides, he is profoundly conversant with the political and military world he is writing about, the discipline is strict; if, like Dionysius in his history of early Rome, the surrounding atmosphere is vague and literary, the resulting

---

[28] *Or.* 5–6, two speeches for and against a proposal to send additional forces to Sicily in 413, are designed to supply the debate 'omitted' by Thuc. 7.16; they draw on Nicias' letter (Thuc. 7. 11–15) and on the debates in Book 6. The recent valuable edition by J. Pernot (1981) provides the first detailed commentary on any work of this kind.

[29] *RG* VIII.170, 12.   [30] I.e. Thuc. 1.68ff, 1.80ff.

[31] On the thorny subject of the interpretation of Thuc. 1.22, see the recent discussion by de Ste Croix (1972) 7–16, with Appendix III.

orations are freer and, in a bad sense, more 'rhetorical'.[32] Polybius' criticism of Timaeus is relevant here:[33] public speeches, exhortations and ambassadorial speeches give 'the main headings' of historical events and make the whole narrative coherent; Timaeus' disregard for truth and insistence on 'what ought to have been said' make him not a historian, but a school rhetor exhibiting his skill on a set theme. The rhetor's work is subject to no real discipline of fact. For him, the situation is in shadow; the light falls only on his own arguments and those which he considers he has to answer. However much our declaimers hunt through the historians and orators for hints, their finished products are self-contained. Like the writers of imaginary letters[34] – another favourite genre of the Second Sophistic – they have no overall plan or conception to satisfy. The most they do in this direction is, like Aristides in the 'Leuctrian' speeches, to plan a set of interrelated speeches.

5

Nevertheless, the question how far the rhetors regarded themselves as restricted by the historical record is a significant one. There was a wide range of attitudes. Some, like Aelius Aristides, took a close interest in the details of historical situations; others indulged in quite wild fantasy. There is some reason to think that a change of attitude took place in the early Empire; it may well be that the 'improvements' in the schools which led to the rejection of some Hellenistic stylistic features and of some moral improprieties also entailed a more responsible attitude to classical history. Stories like the accusation of Aristides for desertion at Salamis,[35] or the charge of ingratitude against Cimon for killing his rich wife[36] do not seem to have parallels later. And in Hermogenes at least we have a strong condemnation of anachro-

---

[32] E.g. Dion. Hal. *Ant. Rom.* 3.22f, 4.39f, 4.48f.
[33] Polyb. 12.25a, cf above ch. 1, n. 81.
[34] The best general account of this literature is still J. Sykutris, 'Epistolographie', *RE* Suppl. 5, 185–220; but see also, e.g. Düring (1951) and Gösswein (1975), both of whom provide useful introductory remarks in their editions of 'Chion' and 'Euripides' respectively.
[35] Demetrius 238.   [36] Sen. *Contr.* 9.1.

nisms and incongruities.[37] It was 'bad invention' (*kakoplaston*) to propose that Cleon should go out to Sicily to help Nicias, when he had been dead for some years, or to mention the battle of Chaeronea in a speech concerned with the earlier capture of Olynthus. The life of Themistocles, in which historical and fictitious elements were inextricably mixed, offers another instance. Some Themistoclean themes involved the story that he was disowned by his father Neocles; this is itself probably unhistorical, and it is significant that Plutarch does not use it, but it was widely accepted and may count as a part of the tradition.[38] When Libanius[39] goes further, however, and makes Neocles claim his son back after Salamis, when he was an *aristeus*, he seems to be going contrary to tradition, if Plutarch[40] is right in saying that 'Neocles did not live to see Themistocles' Salamis'. It was also thought *kakoplaston* to operate with grossly inappropriate legal or social conditions. It was wrong to make Alcibiades[41] act as though the supposed Spartan Law of the Full Moon was valid for Athens also. Similarly, an Athenian setting allowed one to treat foreigners as a desirable tax-paying class of the community, whereas in Sparta the expulsion of aliens was just (*dikaion*). But this raises a moral problem: is it really 'just', and, if not, is it right for the rhetor to represent it as 'just' in the exercises he gives his impressionable pupils? Always alert to such charges, the rhetors have an answer: it is the business of oratory to deal not in absolute justice, but in the specific concepts of individual societies. Once again, the moralizing ps.-Dionysius comes to mind: his insistence on a positive moral tendency seems a response to this kind of subjectivism.

Aristides' most famous set of declamations, the 'Leuctrian' speeches,[42] show how difficult it is to determine the degree of historical fidelity at which a declaimer aims. These are highly sophisticated speeches. There are five of them, supposed to be

[37] 33–4 Rabe.
[38] Thus it is in Nepos' life (*Themistocles* 1).   [39] *Decl.* 9–10.
[40] *Mor.* 496F: οὐκ ἐπεῖδε τὴν Σαλαμῖνα Νεοκλῆς τὴν Θεμιστοκλέους.
[41] *RG* IV.72 (Syrianus). The allusion is to the Spartan excuse for not coming in time to Marathon, Herodotus 6.106.
[42] *Or.* 11–15 (= 33–37 Dindorf).

delivered in the debate at Athens after Leuctra, when both Spartan and Theban ambassadors pleaded for help. Two speeches are by supporters of each side, and one is a plea for neutrality. None of the speakers is named, though they are effectively characterized. Now there are no names in Xenophon's account,[43] nor in all probability were there in that of Ephorus.[44] But Aristides seems to have passed over the names provided in a classical speech,[45] where Kallistratos and Xenokleides are named as supporters of Sparta and Thebes respectively. Other rhetors know other names: Sopatros,[46] outlining the same subject, and knowing Aristides' treatment, mentions Chabrias for the Thebans, Conon for the Spartans, and Iphicrates for neutrality. Of these, Conon was dead; his inclusion is therefore decidedly *kakoplaston*. Chabrias' name may have been suggested by his subsequent trial, and Iphicrates' because he was known to have commanded the force actually sent to help Sparta – though it may seem an odd choice to have made him the advocate of neutrality. This is therefore unintelligent fiction. Aristides' suppression of names is more subtle; and it may perhaps be compared with one of his 'epic' declamations, the 'Embassy to Achilles', in which he takes the situation of *Iliad* IX but never makes it quite clear whether or not he intends his speaker to be thought of as Odysseus.[47] In the 'Leuctrians', the lack of names is perhaps less striking than another odd feature, the absence of the best-known argument deployed in the debate. This was the Spartans' emphasis, not on their own past services to Athens, but on the help they had themselves received from her. To remind people of their kindness to oneself is a more effective plea than asking for their gratitude; the point was recorded by the historian Callisthenes and taken up by Aristotle.[48] Why should a declaimer not use such a good moral sentiment? Perhaps just because it was well known, and the game was to go for something new.

The density of Aristides' reasoning, and the exactness of his

---

[43] *Hellenica* 6.5.33ff.
[44] Cf Diod. 15.65.
[45] [Demosth.] 59.26.
[46] *RG* IV.765 = 5.187.
[47] *Or.* 16 (= 52D); Kindstrand (1973) 215ff.
[48] Callisthenes: *FGrHist* 124F8–13; Aristotle, *EN* 1124b16.

imitation of classical models, may be seen in almost any passage of these closely-knit speeches. Here, as a specimen, is a portion of the argument of the first speaker on the Theban side, emphasizing the honourableness of his cause, and comparing Theban and Spartan 'character':[49]

I could have wished that you had taken part in the battle at Leuctra. You would never have been sharers in a more noble action, nor in one in which you might more properly have taken pride. But I think that, in fact, the present situation has in a sense turned out as it should. The dangers, as I perceive them, are less, but your honour is no less gratified. There would have been nothing surprising in the Thebans' asking for help at the outset, but it is a great thing, an honourable thing, and a thing in which I for my part take much pleasure, that they have not ceased to crave your help when they have had a success such that they could not have hoped for a greater.

I shall not hesitate to say that it seems better to me to help them now that they have asked than to do so unsummoned. In that case, they might have been able to say later that they did not need you, but now that they are here in person and have courted you just as much as the unfortunate do, they could never deny a fact when their own action would refute them. Some say the Thebans are without sense,[50] and in some ways this may be right, but there is one almost universal mistake which they have not made: whereas people who have been confidently believed to be wise lose their heads when they have unhoped for success, the Thebans, after their great victory, have kept at a safe distance from any such mistake. Is it not wisdom in them to come to you and to realize that, if they defeat the Lacedaemonians ten times over, it does them no good, while you are not with them? Nor will the Lacedaemonians have just cause of complaint against you, if you take the Theban part. Let them consider what their decisions were in the case of Aegina and Potidaea. If they will look at this honestly, they will realize that they cannot themselves say otherwise, or cast any other vote, than that you cannot let them be or relax your efforts. Even to-day they cannot prove against you, or charge you with having done,

[49] *Or.* 12 (= 34D), 4–9.
[50] ἀναίσθητοι. The Boeotians were traditionally stupid ([Dion. Hal.] 379. 3 U.–R.: Ἕλλην Βοιωτός· εὐήθης, in a list of standard characters). Cf the interpretation of the proverbial Βοιωτία ὗς ('Boeotian pig') in the paroemiographers: Βοιωτία ὗς· ἐπὶ τῶν ἀναισθήτων καὶ ἀπαιδεύτων (Macarius 2.79 [2.151 Leutsch–Schneidewin]).

any wrong to them in those old days. They demanded that we should give up Aegina and abandon Potidaea. It was just like the orders Cleombrotus has been giving to the Thebans! You must realize that there is nothing fairer of face than the Spartans when they want to gain an advantage. Champions of Greece, zealous defenders of liberty they are – when they want to win something on the side! And when we refused to listen – rightly, men of Athens, in defence of our city's pride – they collected all the allies they could and levied war on us. Little did they care about the oaths and the treaty that they had made with us when we captured Euboea. Little did they care for the trophies and the naval battles – and yet who could imagine that, so long as they had these in mind, they would lift a hand against this city? Nor did they give a thought to the challenge we threw down to them, to submit our differences to discussion. All this was trivial, unimportant to them. I say nothing of the annual invasions that followed, the unending devastation of our land and all the individual combats. They exhausted our registers of men, they made our allies rebel or forced them over to their side, till they had stripped Athens bare. In the end they stopped our food convoys, seized our ships, and pulled down our walls with their own hands. O God!

6

Actual departures from known historical tradition are of course extremely common in declamation, even of the most respectable kind. They fall roughly into two categories, easily defined but not mutually exclusive. On the one hand, there are fabricated events, usually trials or proposals for legislation, which never actually occurred but are suggested by something in the record. On the other, there are individualizations of themes which also occur in a general form, with the characters and places not specified. In this second type, what the rhetor does is what Aristotle describes as the comic poet's characteristic procedure of 'putting names at will on characters, after constructing a plot on the basis of probability'.[51]

Examples of the first kind are legion. The counsellor who advised Croesus to cross the Halys is charged with responsibility

---

[51] *Poetics* 1451b12: συστήσαντες γὰρ τὸν μῦθον διὰ τῶν εἰκότων οὕτω τὰ τυχόντα ὀνόματα ἐπιτιθέασι.

for the disasters that followed.[52] Solon, distressed by the grant of a bodyguard to the future tyrant Pisistratus, goes to court to ask that his own laws shall be annulled.[53] Phye is put on trial for 'offences against the public good' for consenting to dress up as Athena and ride with Pisistratus into Athens.[54] The children of Themistocles plead that the walls he built should be pulled down, because the law says there should be no memorial to a traitor; this is a 'figured' theme, because the real purpose of the action is to remind the Athenians of their debt to Themistocles and their subsequent injustice to him.[55] The events of the Peloponnesian War, as reported by Thucydides, gave rise to a large number of themes of this nature. Because Thucydides says that some of the Potidaeans actually ate one another in the great siege, the Athenians are accused – before some Panhellenic court, presumably that of the Amphictyons – of impiety.[56] Archidamus faces trial at home because he took the Spartan army away from Attica in the plague.[57] Pericles is tried because Archidamus spared his lands in the invasion.[58] Pericles proposes the devastation of Attica – a 'burnt earth' policy, quite unhistorical – and Nicias, to defeat the proposal, moves that the destruction should begin with the holy ground of Eleusis.[59] The rejection of the extreme measure entails the rejection also of the more moderate.

Fourth-century history, and especially the period reflected in the speeches of Demosthenes and Aeschines, was even richer in hints which could be taken up in this way. Many of the 126 themes listed in Kohl's collection are precisely of this kind.[60] A few examples may again suffice to show the nature of the declaimers' art. Aristocrates is put on trial after the revolt of the Chersonese, because this is seen as a direct consequence of his proposal, known from Demosthenes, to outlaw anyone who should kill the mercenary commander Charidemus.[61] Python is tried 'for

---

[52] Syrianus 2.148 Rabe (Kohl [1915] n. 20).
[53] Philostratus, *VS* 542 (a theme by Polemon).
[54] Hermogenes 104.16 Rabe. [55] *RG* v.44.
[56] [Liban.] *Decl.* 13, Thuc. 2.70. [57] *RG* iv.241, 662, 680; Thuc. 2.57.
[58] Hermogenes 141.19 Rabe; Thuc. 2.13.
[59] Apsines 236.23 Sp.–H. [60] Kohl (1915) nos. 203–328.
[61] Apsines 230.19 Sp.–H.; Demosth. 23.100.

crimes against Greece' after Philip's death because, having sought Athenian citizenship when he was in danger after killing the Thracian king Cotys, he subsequently took Philip's part.[62] Demosthenes' 'False Embassy' speech in particular provided good material. In one passage of this,[63] we learn how the Athenians, dismayed by the fate of Phocis, absented themselves from the Pythian games of 346, sending no delegation. From this, the late rhetor Marcellinus – probably the same as the author of an extant Life of Thucydides – devised a theme in which the Athenians are accused of impiety, presumably before the Amphictyonic court. In another place,[64] one of the envoys sent to Philip, by name Phrynon, is said to have sent his own adolescent son to satisfy Philip's paederastic desires. He is accordingly charged with procuring. So good a story – like so many – adhered to various names; it is told of Demades and of an unknown Ploution. From the same speech comes the rather similar story of how Philocrates brought Olynthian women refugees to Athens to employ as prostitutes.[65] This, with all the pathos of the sack of Olynthus and the fate of the refugees, became a favourite theme for the schools.

What could be made of the career of Demosthenes can be seen most clearly from Libanius, who was a close student of the orator's technique, and the author of *hypotheseis* to the speeches which survive and make excellent introductions. The corpus of his declamations includes six Demosthenic themes, all developed by imagining legal processes at various points in Demosthenes' career. In one,[66] Hyperides proposes that Demosthenes shall be a public slave, to save him from being handed over to Philip. In another pair,[67] Demosthenes denounces himself, asking permission to die because of the disgrace of Chaeronea; or again[68] he actually asks to be surrendered to Philip. We find him taking

[62] Apsines 231.17 Sp.–H.; Demosth. 23.127.
[63] Demosth. 19.128, *RG* IV.248.
[64] Demosth. 19.230, cf *RG* V.75, with III.677 (Demades) and IV.176 (Ploution). The otherwise unknown 'Ploution' may be a mistake for 'Phrynon'.
[65] Demosth. 19.309 (ἐφ' ὕβρει): *RG* IV.164.
[66] *Decl.* 18, cf Apsines 336.18 Sp.–H.
[67] *Decl.* 19 and 20.
[68] *Decl.* 21.

refuge at the Altar of Mercy;[69] we see him released by Philip and accused then of not taking part in public life.[70] Many of these are stock themes. In particular, the notion – which is entirely unhistorical – that Philip demanded the surrender of Demosthenes after Chaeronea was a great favourite, of which many variants are recorded.[71] The model seems to have been an event of an earlier period – the Spartan demand for the surrender of Pericles, as an Alcmaeonid, in satisfaction of the 'curse of Cylon'.[72]

One of the most interesting instances of this type of fiction is the story of Cephalus and Aristophon, the subject of two declamations in the Libanian corpus.[73] Aeschines had described the boast of Aristophon of Azenia who had been unsuccessfully prosecuted seventy-five times for making unconstitutional proposals, and contrasted him unfavourably with 'Cephalus of old, thought to be the most democratic of men' who had made many proposals and never been challenged once. The rhetors set these two to dispute for a prize for a good life, which was supposed to have been instituted by law. Polemon seems to have used the theme: he is said to have represented Cephalus as having described his own political career 'although there was no offence forcing him to rebut a charge'.

7

Of the other type of fiction which we see in these speeches – the individualization of general *plasmata* – examples are equally ready to hand. The veterans of Marathon ask to be allowed to serve again in the war against Xerxes ten years later.[74] This is the general theme of the *aristeus* who wishes to reject his privilege

[69] *Decl.* 22.
[70] *Decl.* 23.
[71] E.g. Liban. *Decl.* 19, 20, 21, 22, 23; Hermogenes 157 Rabe; Apsines 234.9 Sp.–H.; *RG* VIII.129 (Sopatros).
[72] Thuc. 1.126; Apsines 233.9 Sp.–H.
[73] Liban. *Decl.* 6–7. The passage in Aeschines is *Or.* 3.194; the theme was used by Polemon (*RG* VIII.3); late lexica actually speak of 'Cephalus' as a writer whose speech survives (Foerster, Libanius VI p. 111). Cf above, p. 37.
[74] *RG* VIII.410; Sen. *Contr.* 1.8; Calp. Flacc. 18; Bonner (1949) 88.

of exemption from service. Again, Pericles has received the honour of having a statue of himself erected by the enemy. He is accordingly accused of treason. The story is told also of Hyperides and Demosthenes; and the generalized theme is used by Hermogenes as an example of a case that can be met by an objection to its legality (*paragraphikon*), on the ground that one ought not to judge a man for what others, not within the jurisdiction of the court, have done in his regard.[75] Another example concerns the famous events of 425, the capture of Sphacteria and Cleon's triumph, a favourite scenario of the schools.[76] Nicias, who is in charge of the fortifications, closes the gates and does not allow Cleon and his three hundred prisoners in. This was strict observance of the law which provided that the gates were not to be opened at night. But unfortunate consequences ensued. In one version, the prisoners escape; in another, an enemy force arrives and massacres them. Nicias is naturally blamed. A generalized form of this story is attested in a number of places; it states, without specifying historical circumstances, that three hundred prisoners of war, who have escaped from enemy hands, are refused admittance by a general who insists on the letter of the security regulations, and are massacred before the walls. Despite the difference – the prisoners now are friends, not enemies of the walled city – this theme is almost certainly the inspiration of the specific stories so improbably attached to the events of 425.

Finally, a couple of examples from Libanius. Timon the misanthrope[77] is in love with Alcibiades. Life is not worth living, he 'denounces himself'. This is the same theme as that of the

[75] Hermogenes 44.7 Rabe, and esp. Sopatros' comments, *RG* v.54f: note v.55.4, ἡ τῶν ὀνομάτων ἐναλλαγὴ οὐδεμίαν διαφορὰν ἤνεγκε τῷ εἴδει ('the change of names makes no difference to the type of case').

[76] Apsines 242.9 Sp.–H.; Sen. *Contr.* 5.7; Cic. *Inv.* 2.123; *RG* IV.246, IV.698, V.98, VIII.411 etc.

[77] *Decl.* 12. The story of Timon comes from comedy (Aristophanes, *Lysistrata* 805ff, *Birds* 1547) and so from commentaries on this, and also from historians (Neanthes, *FGrHist* 84F35; Plutarch, *Ant.* 70). It was also the subject of Lucian's *Timon*, which Libanius certainly knew. The type of the 'misanthrope' represented by Timon differs only in minor ways from that of the *dyskolos*.

anonymous miser in love with the prostitute, the subject of another declamation,[78] with a little more specific character in the main personages. Libanius himself explains:

> This is a difficult subject. We have to represent two opposing characters (*ēthē*), the misanthropist and the lover, and ensure that the speech proceeds on the basis of both characteristics, the ideas introduced not disclosing the contradiction between them. The misanthropist must have the larger part, and the self-denunciation must have its place. Attacks on Alcibiades and abuse of his way of life are appropriate both to the lover and to the misanthropist, and are in place throughout the speech.

The ensuing declamation has little historical content. We hear of Callias, Socrates, Alcibiades' family, and some other celebrated people of the time; but they play no part in the events. Essentially, this is a character study, like those we considered in the last chapter; the names make relatively little difference. It has also a considerable moral element; the discourse on the superiority of animal to human life which it contains has philosophical, mainly Cynic, origins.[79]

Similar is the declamation 'on the recall of Lais'.[80] The return of the great hetaira to Corinth has been proposed on the ground that adultery has increased during her absence and she is therefore needed at home; the speaker opposes the proposition. This theme occurs also in a generalized form,[81] and it seems to have been a popular school subject. It gives both scope for general moralizing (in the tradition of the *thesis*) and for humour, often childish and tedious. It cannot be said that this is one of Libanius' better works, but the arguments have ingenuity, and the priggish speaker is well characterized: 'I am ashamed', he begins, 'by Sophrosyne, I am ashamed to see our city in need of counsellors in order to rid itself of vice!' His main concern is for the reputation of Corinth; he does not want to think it may be famous as a city of vice.[82] His

---

[78] *Decl.* 32.
[79] Lovejoy and Boas (1935), 389–420, devote a chapter to ancient views on the superiority of animals to men.
[80] *Decl.* 25.   [81] *RG* VIII.409.
[82] πόλις πορνοβοσκός – 'brothel city' – was Corinth's proverbial repute: οὐ παντὸς ἀνδρὸς ἐς Κόρινθον ἔσθ' ὁ πλοῦς ('not every man can get to Corinth'), or,

ultimate weapon is the innuendo that the proposer of the lady's recall simply wants her for himself. Once again, the historical element is minimal, character and humour are all.

8

Perhaps the nature of these things may become yet clearer if we take one further instance and examine it in rather more detail. The one I have chosen is a specimen of the first of our two categories of fiction – the invention of a trial – though, as we shall see, it has features of the second also. It is the first example worked in Sopatros, so that he gives unusually full instructions, on which we have already had to draw.[83]

Alcibiades has returned victorious to Athens in 408 B.C., after the naval victory at Cyzicus. According to tradition, he was given a golden crown and chosen as General by sea and land; his property was restored and the curses which had been pronounced against him were revoked. The rhetors exploited this historic moment in several ways. We know of declamations in which he proposed to attack Sicily again,[84] and others in which he offended against public feeling by having scenes of the Sicilian disaster depicted on his drinking cups.[85] In the exercise which we are to consider, Alcibiades will defend himself against a charge of attempting tyranny. The situation is stylized in a way quite unjustified by history, but easily explained in terms of declamatory convention. Alcibiades is simply the typical *aristeus*, who has been given the traditional free choice of reward for his valour. He has chosen a bodyguard, and this lays him open to the charge of aiming at tyranny (*epithesis tyrannidos*), since the acquisition of a guard was traditionally the first step on the tyrant's road to power. In Sophistopolis, let us recall, anxious eyes are always on the watch for attempts at *coups d'état*: to promise prisoners freedom, to maintain a body of *apokēryktoi*, to recommend the surrender of personal arms to the general, even to look up at the

in Horace's words (*Epist.* 1.17.36) non cuivis homini contingit adire Corinthum. This declamation can therefore be seen as a discourse on a proverb – an elaborated *progymnasma*.

[83] See above, ch. 3, p. 49, on *stochasmos*.
[84] Apsines 253.12 Sp.–H.
[85] Hermogenes 68 Rabe: cf *RG* IV.74, 6.621.

acropolis with tears in your eyes, are all actions which can motivate a prosecution.[86] It was of course part of the historical tradition that Alcibiades might have become tyrant at this time. Plutarch[87] has a vivid picture, of uncertain provenance, of the ordinary people passionately wanting to be ruled by him, and begging him to 'throw down laws and decrees and the nonsense that is ruining the city' and seize control. This passage has always been a puzzle: the similarity of language between it and some phrases spoken by Callicles in Plato's *Gorgias* raises the suspicion that it is either Plutarch's own invention or an embroidery due to some earlier historian. What we have in Sopatros is the marriage of the historical record, as he perceived it, with the conventions of declamation.

Alcibiades' defence is not easy. Our teacher carefully explains, in elementary terms, how it may be managed. The case is a simple one of fact (*stochasmos haplous*). The way in which the defendant can deny the charge is determined by Alcibiades' known character. He is independent and proud (*authadēs kai megalophrōn*), as we can see from Thucydides' account of his opposition to Nicias and from Plutarch's *Life* – which our teacher clearly expects us to know. We need a good deal of pomp and circumstance (*pompikon*); and this means that we have an opportunity to display skills which are usually more in demand in encomia and invective, that is to say in epideictic oratory, than in declamation. This does not just refer to tone, but to method; so the Hermogenes commentator Sopatros[88] explains that 'encomiastic topics' form the backbone of the treatment of another kindred theme, 'the examination of Alcibiades' qualifications for the office of torch-bearer in the mysteries'.

Alcibiades begins without false modesty. He starts by addressing the audience with almost Ciceronian bravado as 'You who owe your liberty to Alcibiades';[89] and so shows at once both his own consciousness of achievement and his abhorrence of

---

[86] See above, ch. 2, p. 33.
[87] Plutarch, *Alcibiades* 34.7, with Pl. *Gorgias* 484A4, 492C7.
[88] *RG* v.10, cf 6.468 and [Liban.] fr. 50 Foerster.
[89] ἄνδρες οἱ δι' Ἀλκιβιάδην ἐλεύθεροι.

Declamation and history

tyranny. He can also show his greatness of soul (*megalophrosynē*) by confessing to just one mistake in policy in his whole career: his failure to ask for his accuser's death as his hero's reward. We see here with appalling clarity the distortion of history into declamatory fantasy. Synesius' remark[90] is entirely apt: 'What city gives the *aristeus* the right to kill an opponent?' Certainly not the Athens in which Alcibiades lived, for all the wilful and sporadic cruelty that marked its political life. We are back in Sophistopolis.

The introduction (*prooimia*) is followed by the *katastasis*. The points which Alcibiades must try to establish in this selective narrative are these: that he is very proud of his success; that he expects to achieve even more for the city now that he has the means to do so; and that, as a pupil of Socrates, he could not possibly have retained any ambition to be a tyrant. In working out this scheme, the speaker is to follow more or less the chronological order of events, much as they are set out in Plutarch. It is interesting that he rests a part of his case on Socrates' teaching, and says that Socrates showed him 'that democracy is a fine thing'; this recalls the lengthy argument in Libanius' *Apology* intended to demonstrate Socrates' hostility to tyrants and friendliness towards the *dēmos*.[91] Interesting also is Alcibiades' suppression of any mention of the charge of subversion (*dēmou katalysis*) that was made against him in 415,[92] alongside the charges relating to the Hermae and the Eleusinia, which he calls 'stage-managed'.[93] It is natural that he should do this, and good tactics; as also is the strong emphasis he lays on the fact – known from Thucydides – that he asked to be tried before he set sail for Sicily. These omissions and emphases culminate in an extraordinary scene in which Alcibiades watches the approach of the message ship *Salaminia* as she draws near the coast of Sicily, and soliloquizes about his own position.[94] He deliberates about what

[90] Above, ch. 2, n. 1.
[91] Liban. *Apol. Socr.* (= *Decl.* 1) 48–63.
[92] Thuc. 6.61.
[93] δραματουργοῦσιν (p. 5, 1).
[94] This may have been suggested by Liban. *Apol. Socr.* 139, where Alcibiades imagines the Salaminia herself warning him not to return to Athens.

he should do, and concludes by telling himself that it is his duty to escape from the Athenians' anger, which his accusers have succeeded in arousing, in order to do them a greater service in the future. The nature of this service, in Samos and at Cyzicus, is to be the highest point of the entire narrative; what befell at Sparta and elsewhere is naturally entirely omitted.

After the *katastasis*, normal practice requires *elenchōn apaitēsis*, 'demand for proofs', the defendant's natural countermeasure.[95] The rule here is that you should make much of the defects in the prosecution's case and play down its strength. In this case, there are no witnesses to Alcibiades' ambitions – how could there be: He must therefore demand them. Murderers and robbers are never convicted without evidence: why should a supposed subverter of democracy be treated differently? Where are the stores of arms?[96] Where is the bodyguard? Why has not the prison been seized? There is no more reason to charge the defendant than there would be to charge his malicious accuser with the same offence.

The next move is the topic of 'will and means'. Reasons are sure to be advanced why Alcibiades should have wanted to be tyrant. These reasons must be refuted. It will also be said that he *could* have done it; this cannot be directly refuted for it is undeniable, but it can be countered by asserting that a rebuttal of the allegation that he 'wanted' despotic power carries with it a refutation of this point also. So the concentration is on 'the will'; it is as though he was saying 'where there is no will, there is no way'. Now there are four reasons why Alcibiades might have wanted absolute power: sheer longing for it, desire for greater honour, wish to punish his enemies, and wish to help his friends. In rebutting these possibilities, the speaker finds ammunition, once again, in the so-called 'topics of encomium': education, actions and family connections all afford arguments. He was taught by Socrates what the best constitution was – and it was certainly not tyranny. He did not attempt to make the Spartans set him up at Athens as tyrant, though they might have done so; indeed he himself restored democratic rule after the

[95] Cf ch. 3, p. 45.   [96] Perhaps read τὰς πανοπλίας, p. 9, 6.

Revolution of 411. And consider his family associations. Pericles achieved power by being 'popular' (*dēmotikos*) and Alcibiades would not wish to be outshone by him. Xanthippus, his chief model, killed a tyrant and produced good laws. His own father, Clinias, fought at Artemisium and died heroically at Coronea.

Here there is a historical absurdity. Who ever heard such a thing of Pericles' father, Xanthippus? True, he married Agariste, and had links therefore with Cleisthenes and the establishment of democracy after the Pisistratids had been expelled. But he had no part in all this himself. The explanation is simple and discreditable. Sopatros has made a howler: he misunderstood a passage of Plutarch by falsely taking Xanthippus and not Cleisthenes as the antecedent of a relative clause.[97]

All this tends to show that the first possible reason for Alcibiades' having planned the attempt – sheer desire – is invalid. And this conclusion can be confirmed by elaborating on the well-known horrors of the tyrant's position, his perpetual fears and anxieties. Even if he had had the desire, there is a further consideration that would have stopped him: the thought of the rewards awaiting anyone who assassinates a tyrant. No one would voluntarily put himself into a position in which there was a price on his head. So we turn to the second possible reason, that he may have sought greater honour. Impossible: how could he achieve greater success and renown than the battles at Cyzicus and in the Hellespont have already given him?

Thirdly: perhaps he wanted to help his friends. The same sort of consideration disposes of this also. His present situation puts him in a position to do anything he likes for them.

As for the fourth motive – desire to punish enemies – this is met by the fact that, though he might have asked for his accuser's death, he has not done so. Here, once again, Alcibiades fades into the stock figure of the *aristeus* who can choose what reward he will.

---

[97] *RG* VIII. 11.17: τυραννοκτονήσας καὶ νόμους καὶ ἀρίστην τὴν πολιτείαν κατέστησεν derives from Plutarch, *Pericles* 2.2 (where Cleisthenes is the antecedent of the relative): ὃς ἐξήλασε Πεισιστρατίδας καὶ κατέλυσε τὴν τυραννίδα γενναίως καὶ νόμους ἔθετο καὶ πολιτείαν ἄριστα κεκραμένην...κατέστησεν.

When these arguments have been disposed of, the speaker turns to the prosecution's contention that his choice of a bodyguard implies the aim of tyranny. This he answers by two moves, *antilēpsis* and *chrōma*.[98] The first points out that the act of which the prosecution complains, namely his choice, is perfectly legal; the law lays no restriction on the *aristeus*' freedom of choice. The second explains the motive for his request: it is the existence of enemies, envious of his success, and these are even more numerous now than they were before his victories.

We are moving now towards the end. This is a case where a 'persuasive defence' (*pithanē apologia*) can be made. It consists in suggesting that, if Alcibiades had seriously wanted to be a tyrant, he would have avoided making his particular choice of reward. The argument is an analogy. Murderers do not carry their bloodstained weapons, poisoners do not advertise their possession of lethal drugs.

As often, this 'defence' leads into the epilogue, here no mere recapitulation, nor merely emotional, but summarizing the defendant's position both from the point of view of his own desire for honour and his family tradition of patriotism, and from the point of view of the public interest. It is both just and expedient to acquit him: just, because the accuser deserves punishment; expedient, in order to avoid giving pleasure to the city's enemies, and to secure Alcibiades' future services.

Finally: 'I will use my bodyguard against the Spartans. Let us launch the fleet. I will reconquer Sicily, subdue Italy, and make Athens mistress of the world.'

Thus does declamation marry history with fantasy, ingenuity with childishness, wit with folly.

[98] Cf above, ch. 3, p. 49.

Bibliography

ABBREVIATIONS

CGL	*Corpus glossariorum Latinorum*, ed. G. Götz, Leipzig 1888–1923.
FGrHist.	F. Jacoby, *Fragmente der griechischen Historiker*, Leiden 1955–1969.
PLRE	A. H. M. Jones, J. R. Martindale and J. Morris, *The Prosopography of the Later Roman Empire*, vol. I, Cambridge 1971; vol. II, 1980.
RE	Pauly-Wissowa, *Realenzyklopädie der classischen Altertumswissenschaft*, Stuttgart 1890–
RG	C. Walz, *Rhetores Graeci* I–IX, Stuttgart 1832–1836 (repr. Osnabrück 1968).
RLM	*Rhetores Latini Minores*, ed. C. Halm, Leipzig 1863 (repr. Frankfurt 1964).
Sp.	L. Spengel, *Rhetores Graeci*, I–III, Leipzig 1853.
Sp.–H.	L. Spengel–C. Hammer, *Rhetores Graeci*, I.2, Leipzig 1884.

EDITIONS

Aelius Aristides, vol. I (*Or.* 1–16), ed. F. W. Lenz and C. A. Behr, Leiden 1976–1980; vol. II (*Or.* 17–53) ed. B. Keil, Berlin 1898.

Ammonius, *De adfinium vocabulorum differentia*, ed. K. Nickau, Leipzig 1966.

Anonymus Seguierianus: in *Rhetores Graeci* I.2, ed. L. Spengel and C. Hammer; also ed. C. Graeven, *Cornuti Artis Rhetoricae Epitome*, Berlin 1891.

Antiphon, *Tetralogies*, ed. F. Decleva Caizzi, Milan 1969.

Aristaenetus, ed. O. Mazal, Stuttgart 1971.

Calpurnius Flaccus, ed. L. Håkanson, Stuttgart 1978.

Choricius, ed. R. Foerster and E. Richtsteig, Leipzig 1929 (repr. Stuttgart 1972).

Dionysius of Halicarnassus, *Opuscula*, ed. H. Usener and L. Radermacher, Leipzig (vol. I) 1899, (vol. II) 1904.
Ennodius, ed. F. Vogel, *Mon. Germ. Hist.*, *Auct. Ant.*, VII, Berlin 1885.
Hermagoras, ed. D. Matthes, Leipzig 1962.
Hermogenes, ed. H. Rabe, Stuttgart 1913.
Herodes Atticus (?), *Peri Politeias*, ed. U. Albini, Florence 1968.
Himerius, ed. A. Colonna, Rome 1951; ed. G. Wernsdorf, Göttingen 1790.
Iamblichus, *Babyloniaca*, ed. E. Habrich, Leipzig 1960.
Lesbonax, ed. F. Kiehr, Leipzig 1907.
Libanius, ed. R. Foerster, 12 vols., Leipzig 1903–1923.
'Longinus', *On the Sublime*, ed. D. A. Russell, Oxford 1964.
Lucian, ed. M. D. Macleod, Oxford 1972–1979; ed. F. Jacobitz, Leipzig 1851.
Macarius: in *Corpus Paroemiographorum Graecorum*, ed. E. Leutsch and F. Schneidewin, Göttingen 1839 (reprint, 1958).
Marcus Diaconus, *Vita Porphyrii*, ed. 'societatis philologae Bonnensis sodales', Leipzig 1895.
Menander Rhetor, ed. D. A. Russell and N. G. Wilson, Oxford 1981.
Philostratus, *Lives of the Sophists*, ed. W. C. Wright, Loeb Classical Library, London and Cambridge, Mass. 1921.
Polemon, ed. H. Hinck, Leipzig 1873.
Quintilian, *Institutio Oratoria*, ed. M. Winterbottom, Oxford 1970.
[Quintilian] *Declamationes Minores*, ed. C. Ritter, Leipzig 1884.
  Declamationes Maiores, ed. G. Lehnert, Leipzig 1905.
Seneca, *Controversiae and Suasoriae*, ed. M. Winterbottom, Loeb Classical Library, 1974; ed. H. J. Müller, Vienna 1887.
  Suasoriae, ed. W. A. Edward, Cambridge 1928.
Stobaeus, ed. C. Wachsmuth and O. Hense, Berlin 1884–1912.
Synesius, *Opuscula*, ed. N. Terzaghi, Rome 1944.
Syrianus, *Commentaria in Hermogenem*, ed. H. Rabe, Leipzig 1892–3 (also cited from *RG*).
Zenobius, *see* Macarius.

BOOKS AND ARTICLES REFERRED TO BY AUTHOR AND DATE ONLY

Barwick, K. *Das rednerische Bildungsideal Ciceros* (= *Abh. d. sächs. Akademie der Wissenschaften, phil.-hist. kl.* LIV.3), Berlin 1963.
Blum, H. *Die antike Mnemotechnik* (= Spudasmata XV), Hildesheim 1969.

Bibliography

Bompaire, J. *Lucien écrivain* (= Bibl. des écoles françaises d'Athènes et de Rome CXC), Paris 1958.
Bonner, S. F. *Roman Declamation*, Liverpool 1949.
    Roman Education, London 1977.
Bornecque, H. *Les déclamations et les déclamateurs d'après Sénèque le père* (= Travaux et mémoires de l'Université de Lille N.S., 1.1), Lille 1902.
Boulanger, A. *Aelius Aristide* (= Bibl. des écoles françaises d'Athènes et de Rome CXXVI), Paris 1923.
Bowersock, G. W. *Augustus and the Greek World*, Oxford 1965.
    Greek Sophists in the Roman Empire, Oxford 1969.
    (ed.) *Approaches to the Second Sophistic* (Publ. of the American Philological Association), University Park, Pennsylvania 1974.
    Julian the Apostate, London 1978.
Bowie, E. L. 'The importance of sophists', *Yale Classical Studies* XXVII (1982).
Brink, C. O. *Horace on Poetry: the 'Ars Poetica'*, Cambridge 1971.
Burgess, R. C. *Epideictic Literature*, Chicago 1902 (repr. Ann Arbor and London 1980).
Clark, D. L. *Rhetoric in Greco-Roman Education*, New York 1957.
Clarke, E. D. *Travels in Various Countries*, vol. V, London 1817.
Corbett, P. E. *The Roman Law of Marriage*, Oxford 1969.
de Decker, J. *Juvenalis Declamans* (= Université de Gand, Recueil de Travaux...fasc. 41), Ghent 1913.
de Falco, V. *Demade oratore: testimonianze e frammenti*, Naples 1954.
de Ste Croix, G. E. M. *The Origins of the Peloponnesian War*, London 1972.
de Vries, G. J. *Commentary on the Phaedrus of Plato*, Amsterdam 1969.
Dover, K. J. *Lysias and the Corpus Lysiacum*, Berkeley and Los Angeles 1968.
Düring, I. *Herodicus the Cratetean*, Stockholm 1941.
    Chion of Heraclea, Göteborg 1951 (repr. 1979).
Fairweather, J. *Seneca the Elder*, Cambridge 1981.
Gösswein, H.-U. *Die Briefe des Euripides* (= Beiträge zur klassischen Philologie LV), Meisenheim-am-Glan 1975.
Grube, G. M. A. *Demetrius: A Greek Critic*, Toronto 1961.
Hagedorn, D. *Zur Ideenlehre des Hermogenes* (= Hypomnemata VIII), Göttingen 1964.
Harrison, A. R. W. *The Law of Athens: the Family and Property*, Oxford **1968.**

Heldmann, K. *Antike Theorien über Entwicklung und Verfall der Redekunst* (= Zetemata LXXVII), Munich 1982.
Hillyard, B. P. *Commentary on Plutarch: De audiendo*, Arno Press, New York 1981.
Hunger, H. *Die Hochsprachliche profane Literatur der Byzantiner* (= Handbuch der Altertumswissenschaft XII.5.1), Munich 1978.
Jander, K. *Oratorum et rhetorum graecorum nova fragmenta*, Bonn 1913.
Jäneke, W. *De statuum doctrina ab Hermogene tradita*, diss. Leipzig 1904.
Jüttner, H. *De Polemonis rhetoris vita operibus arte* (*Breslauer philologische Abhandlungen* VIII.1), 1898.
Kennedy, G. A. *The Art of Persuasion in Greece*, Princeton 1963.
  The Art of Rhetoric in the Roman World (*ARRW*), Princeton 1972.
  Classical Rhetoric and its Christian and Secular Tradition, London 1980.
  Greek Rhetoric under Christian Emperors, Princeton 1983.
Kindstrand, J. F. *Homer in der zweiten Sophistik*, Uppsala 1973.
Kohl, R. *De scholasticarum declamationum argumentis ex historia petitis* (= Rhetorische Studien IV), Paderborn 1915.
Lausberg, H. *Handbuch der literarischen Rhetorik*, Munich 1960.
Lossau, M. *Untersuchungen zur antiken Demosthenesausgabe* (= *Palingenesia* II), Bad Homburg and Berlin 1964.
Lovejoy, A. and G. Boas. *Primitivism and Related Ideas in Antiquity*, Baltimore 1935.
Markowski, H. *De Libanio Socratis defensore*, Breslau 1910.
Martin, J. *Antike Rhetorik* (*Handbuch der Altertumswissenschaft* II.3), Munich 1974.
Meinhardt, E. *Perikles bei Plutarch*, diss. Frankfurt 1957.
Morel, W. 'Meletē', in *RE* XV.1.496–9.
Pernot, L. *Les discours siciliens d'Aelius Aristide*, Arno Press, New York 1981.
Radermacher, L. *Artium scriptores* (Sitzungsberichte der Oesterreichische Akademie, phil. hist. klasse CCXXVII.3) Vienna 1951.
Reardon, B. P. *Les courants littéraires grecs des IIe et IIIe siècles*, Paris 1971.
Rohde, E. *Der griechische Roman*, ed. 3, Leipzig 1914.
Russell, D. A. *Criticism in Antiquity*, London 1981.
Schmid, W. *Der Atticismus*, Stuttgart 1887–1896.
Sheppard, A. D. R. *Studies on the 5th and 6th Essays of Proclus' Commentary on the Republic* (Hypomnemata LXI), Göttingen 1980.
Süss, W. *Ethos*, Leipzig and Berlin 1910.
Sussman, L. A. *The Elder Seneca*, Leiden 1978.
Volkmann, R. *Die Rhetorik der Griechen und Römer*, ed. 2, Leipzig 1885.
Winterbottom, M. *Roman Declamation*, Bristol 1980.

Indexes

I GENERAL INDEX

Achilles Tatius 38
Adaios 8
Adrian of Tyre 4, 81
adultery 33ff, 59, 60ff
advocates 14
Aelian 89
Aemilianus 8
Aeschines 18, 35, 118f
Alcibiades 14, 24, 49, 81, 114, 121f, 123ff
Alexander 4, 78, 107
Alexander Peloplaton 84
ambiguity 69
Andocides 17
Antioch 3, 5
Antiphon 17, 40
Antisthenes 16
Apsines 7, 41, 89, 107
Aquila 42
Aristaenetus 80
aristeus 19, 24ff, 97ff, 102ff
Aristides ('the just') 44, 113
Aristides, Aelius 4, 13, 74, 76f, 80, 81, 107, 112f, 117
Aristomenes 24
Aristophanes 94, 97, 100
Artemon 8
Athens 3
athletes 66
audiences 79ff, 84ff

blind man, character in declamation 67

cannibalism, at siege of Potidaea 118
Carponianus 7
Cephalus and Aristophon 37, 120
character (*see ēthos*, Index III), ch. 5 passim
Chariton 38
Charondas 37
Choricius 5, 26, 30, 78, 81, 82f, 102ff

Christian subjects of declamation 12
Cicero 6, 25
Cimon 113
Clarke, E. D. 39
Cleon 63, 114, 121
Cleonnis 24
comedy, source of vocabulary for declamation 110
contemporary references in declamation 108
Crete 33
Croesus 117
Cyzicus 76, 123

Damianus 75
declamation (*see also meletē*): influence on literature 2f; hostile criticism of 21ff; passes as genuine oratory 111
Demades 111
Demetrius of Phalerum 18
Demetrius, *On Style* 20
Demosthenes 118ff
Dinarchus 11
Dionysius of Halicarnarsus 112
ps.–Dionysius, *Art of Rhetoric* 7, 13, 71ff, 88, 114
Dorion 8

Eleusis 53ff
encomium 126
Epicurus 107
Eunapius 5
Evagoras 42

Favorinus 52
fees charged by teachers of declamation 74
Flamininus 107
forensic speeches by declaimers 12f

Gaza 3, 6

Gorgias (sophist) 16, 75, 79, 106, 109
Gorgias (writer on figures) 8
Greek and Latin, differences between in practice of declamation 106

Heliodorus (novelist) 23, 38
helpful friends, theme in comedy and declamation 92, 99
Hermagoras of Temnos 6, 43
Hermagoras (younger) 9, 27
Hermogenes 6, 43ff, 53ff, 87
Herodes Atticus 12, 84, 109, 111
Herodotus 15, 24
Himerius 5, 29, 107
Hippias 75, 109
Hippodamos 37
Hippodromos 75
historians, speeches in 112
history, use of in declamation ch. 6, passim
Homer 15, 110
Hyperides 110, 119

imitation of Attic style 71, 109

Jonson, Ben 5
juries, size of 16, 23
Juvenal 2

Lais 122
laws, invented by declaimers 37f
lecture-halls 76
Leptines 4, 107
Lesbocles 9
Lesbonax 4, 81
letters, imaginary 113
Leuctra, Battle of 114f
Libanius 5, 13, 15, 21, 27, 31, 37, 45, 65, 77, 81, 88ff, 91ff, 108, 110, 122
Lollianus 74, 107, 108
love, as theme in declamation 25f, 102f
Lucan 2
Lucian 4, 7, 76, 78, 82
Lycurgus (orator) 42
Lysias 17, 88

Marcellinus 44
Massilia 36
Maximus of Tyre 38, 78
meletē (*see also* 'declamation'): distinguished from other rhet.

exercises 10f; sources of, in Greek literature 15f
Menander (comic poet) 89
Menander Rhetor 10
Menelaus 110
Mikon (painter) 56f
mime 39
Minucianus 6, 7, 42
misanthropist (*dyskolos*) 36, 89ff
misers 14, 96ff, 102ff
Mysteries (of Eleusis) 53

Nicephorus Basilakes 12
Nicetes (mentioned in Seneca) 9
Nicetes (of Smyrna) 13, 19
Nicias 86, 121
novel, relation to declamation 38
note-taking by audience 80

Odysseus 110
Olympia 66
Olynthus 119
oracles 70
Ovid 2, 12

painters, subject of declamation 56
papyri, as evidence for declamation 4
parents and children, conflict between, in declamation (cf Index III s.v. *apokēryxis*) 30ff, 59ff, 62, 64, 102ff
Pericles 111, 121f, 127
Petronius 26
Philagros 80
Philostratus 8, 18, ch. 4 passim
Phrynon 119
Phye 118
Plato 15, 24
Plutarch 24, 124
Polemon (of Laodicea) 4, 58, 81, 82, 111
Polybius 20, 113
Potidaea 118
preliminary speech before delivery of declamation (cf *dialexis* in Index III) 77
Proclus of Naucratis 75, 109
prostitution, theme in declamation 35

Quintilian 18, 31, 40

rape, theme in declamation 35, 67
'rapist's choice' 34

General index

Rich Man and Poor Man, conflict between 14, 19, 21, 27ff

sacrilege, theme in declamation 51
Scopelianus 13, 75, 77, 82
Scythians, subject of declamation 85
self-denunciation, *see prosangelia in* Index III
Seneca, L. Annaeus 1ff, 26, 44
Severus (rhetor) 12
shorthand 80
Smyrna 76
Socrates 16, 108
Solon 118
Sopatros (e.g.) 7, 11, 36, 42, 45, 47ff, 53ff, 72, 108, 115, 123ff
sophists, personality of 82 (and ch. 4, passim)
sorcerer (*magos*), character in declamation 26
stasis, importance of, e.g. 40ff (*and see* Index III)

stratēgos ('general'), character in declamation 22f, 51, 64
style, Sopatros' comments on 72
Synesius 21, 125
Syrianus 7, 42, 44

Tacitus 108
talkative wife, theme of declamation 91ff
Telephus of Pergamum 41
Themistocles 14, 114ff, 118
Theophrastus 94
Thucydides 16, 58, 81, 112, 118
Timon 121f
tyrants and tyrannicides 19, 32f, 45ff, 123ff

Valerius Maximus 35

witnesses and arguments, relative value of, 45

II INDEX OF PRINCIPAL PASSAGES DISCUSSED

AESCHINES
  De falsa legatione 49   100
ARISTIDES, AELIUS
  Or. 5–6   112
  11–15   114f
  12. 4–9   116
  51. 29–34   76
CHORICIUS
  Decl. 5 and 6 (pp. 224ff F.–R.)   102ff
  Dialexis 12 (p. 248)   83
  21 (p. 382)   78
DIODORUS SICULUS
  12.17–18   37
DIONYSIUS OF HALICARNASSUS
  Dinarchus 11   111
ps.–DIONYSIUS
  Ars rhetorica pp. 359ff U.–R.   2
  pp. 365ff U.–R.   71ff
HELIODORUS
  Aethiopica 1.14.1   23
HERMOGENES (ed. Rabe)
  pp. 32ff   43
  pp. 37ff   55
  pp. 43ff   44ff
  pp. 59ff   52ff
  pp. 65ff   56ff
  p. 76   63
  pp. 79ff   60
  pp. 82ff   65ff
  pp. 90ff   69
HIMERIUS
  Or. 1   110
  Or. 4   29
LIBANIUS
  Decl. 6–7   120
  12   121f
  15–16   37
  25   122
  26   91ff
  27.3–8   89
  33   97ff
  Narrationes 26 (8.49 F.)   92
  Epist. 405   77
[LIBANIUS]
  Decl. 34   58
OLYMPIODORUS
  In Gorgiam, ed. Westerink, 71.3   65

Indexes

OVID		8.2ff	123ff
Epist. ex Ponto		8.7	45
1.5.5–6	86	8.10	47
		8.13	49f
PHILOSTRATUS		8.110ff	53ff
Vitae Sophistarum 481	18	8.126ff	56ff
526–7	108	8.170	112
528	78	8.244ff	59ff
571–4	84	8.247ff	60ff
579	80	8.325	108
583	80	8.336–7	64f
604	75	8.349ff	66
		8.362ff	67ff
PLUTARCH		8.370ff	67
Pericles 202	127	8.377ff	69
Moralia 319B	24	STOBAEUS (ed. Wachsmuth-Hense)	
QUINTILIAN		4.40.22	13
2.4.41	18	SUETONIUS	
		De rhetoribus 30	35
'RHETORES GRAECI' (ed. Walz)		*Nero* 20	85
		SYNESIUS	
(References between 8.2 and 8.385 are to Sopatros' *Diaireseis*)		*De insomniis* 20	21
		VALERIUS MAXIMUS	
1.466	12	2.6.8	35
4.469	28	VIRGIL	
4.843ff	69	*Georgics* 1.259ff	99

III INDEX OF TECHNICAL TERMS

This list gives brief explanations of the main rhetorical terms used in this book. It is not intended as a guide to the sense of these words in other contexts. Greek rhetorical terminology is notoriously fluid and inconsistent. The lack of a modern lexicon to replace J. G. T. Ernesti's *Lexicon Technologiae Graecorum Rhetoricae* (Leipzig 1795, repr. Hildesheim 1962) has not been made good by the handbooks (Volkmann, Lausberg, Martin), though much information may be found in these and in the indexes of modern editions of rhetorical texts.

Amphibolia (ἀμφιβολία): ambiguity, a legal issue (*nomikē stasis*, q.v.) 69
anaphōnēsis (ἀναφώνησις): a voice exercise 9
antenklēma (ἀντέγκλημα): 'counter-charge', when the defendant makes an accusation against the prosecutor or someone else; not always clearly distinguished from *metastasis* (q.v.) 7 n. 24, 17 n. 72, 58, 61
anthorismos (ἀνθορισμός): 'counter-definition' (cf *horos*) 52, 54
antilēpsis (ἀντίληψις)
    (i) 'counter-hold'; a term often used of a defendant's rebuttal of the accusation on the ground that 'he has done nothing forbidden'; the answer is a *metalēpsis* (q.v.), in which the prosecution alleges (e.g.) that in the particular circumstances the action must be regarded as forbidden (cf *antiparastasis*) 48, 128.

Technical terms

(ii) as a *stasis*, Lat. *constitutio iuridicialis absoluta* in which the defendant admits the deed but denies it is an offence 56, 97

antinomia (ἀντινομία): 'conflict of laws', a type of *nomikē stasis* (q.v.) 67

antiparastasis (esp. in phrase κατ' ἀντιπαράστασιν): 'rejoinder'; as a type of answer to a defendant's *antilēpsis* (q.v.), this is not a straight denial (*enstasis*, q.v.) but an assertion that, given the cirumstances, the act *is* a forbidden one 48

antistasis (ἀντίστασις): a defendant's argument, alleging that what he did, so far from being a crime was beneficial (cf *chrōma*) 7 n. 24, 42, 57, 58, 59, 66

antithesis (ἀντίθεσις)
   (i) an objection stated by the speaker in order that he may himself offer a refutation (*lysis*) of it 64, 95
   (ii) as a *stasis*, Lat. *constitutio iuridicialis adsumptiva*, i.e. the type of case in which the defendant admits that he has done wrong but defends himself by *antistasis*, *antenklēma*, *metastasis* or *syngnōmē* (qq.v.) 56, 58
   (iii) a counter-charge as a move in defence 52

ap' archēs achri telous (ἀπ' ἀρχῆς ἄχρι τέλους): lit. 'from beginning to end', a move in which the prosecutor (or sometimes the defendant) argues from an acknowledged event to the fact which he wishes to establish; in practice, a detailed and strongly angled narrative of the events leading up to the trial 47, 59

aperistatos (ἀπερίστατος) 'uncircumstantial' 44

apheles logos (ἀφελής λόγος): 'simple style'; i.e. writing of an informal and generally non-periodic kind, opposed to the style of formal oratory (*politikos logos*) 78

apokēryxis, apokēryktos (ἀποκήρυξις, ἀποκήρυκτος: Lat. *abdicatio, abdicatus*): a (largely unhistorical) legal process of 'disowning' a son, by which the father deprives the 'disowned' of all rights in the family 31, 101, 123

asystatos (ἀσύστατος): 'non-constituted', i.e. 'not amounting to a proper case', a term used of badly devised declamation-themes (cf *kakoplaston*) 43

biaios horos (βίαιος ὅρος): 'forcible definition', a term for a move in which the speaker throws his opponent's interpretation of the facts back at him, showing that it really assists his own case (cf *pithanē apologia*) 59

boulēsis kai dynamis (βούλησις καὶ δύναμις): discussion of a defendant's 'wish and ability' (i.e. motive and opportunity) to perform the act of which he is accused 46, 126

chrōma (χρῶμα: Lat. *color*): 'colour' or 'gloss': especially a move made by a defendant to give a justifiable reason for his action, e.g. by explaining that he did it with honourable intentions (cf *metathesis aitias*) 57, 128

controversia: the Latin term for a forensic declamation, i.e. one in which the speaker takes one side of an imagined law-suit 4, 85, 106

controversia de genere: Latin term for a case belonging to the *stasis* of 'quality' (see *poiotēs*) 55

dēmosion adikēma (δημόσιον ἀδίκημα): 'public offence', i.e. an offence caused by dereliction or obstruction of public duty, usually (but not necessarily) committed by someone in an official position 56

diairesis (διαίρεσις): 'division', esp. the division of a case into its constituent arguments. (Sopatros' *diaireseis* , it should be noted, include *prooimia*, narrative and epilogue, i.e. some of the 'parts' of a speech, as well as the 'headings' (*kephalaia*) which Hermogenes prescribes) ch. 3, passim

dialexis (διάλεξις): 'talk', esp. the preliminary informal talk preceding the delivery of a declamation or other major speech (cf *lalia, theoria*) 75, 77, 83, 85

dikaiologia (δικαιολογία): any issue of right or expediency relating to the past (and so belonging to forensic oratory, not to deliberative, which is about the future); in Hermogenes, the main category of *logikai staseis* (q.v.) subdivided into *antilēpsis* and *antithesis* (qq.v.) 56

ekphrasis (ἔκφρασις): 'description', whether as an element in a speech or as a separate *progymnasma* (q.v.) 30

elenchōn apaitēsis (ἐλέγχων ἀπαίτησις): 'demand for proofs'; a move which may be made by either side for the other party to produce evidence or a reasoned case, the object being to embarrass the opponent by always asking for whichever kind of proof (witnesses or reasons of probability) cannot be had 45, 126

emphasis (ἔμφασις): 'innuendo' 110

empiptōn (ἐμπίπτων): 'incidental', used of a *stochasmos* or *horos* (qq.v.) which arises in the course of the main argument of a case 50, 53

enstasis (ἔνστασις): 'objection': total denial of a charge (contrast *antiparastasis*, q.v.) 48

epideictic (ἐπιδεικτικός: Lat. *demonstrativus*): name applied to the third main branch of rhetoric, distinct from the 'forensic' and 'deliberative' branches (cf *controversia, suasoria*); it covers primarily the oratory of praise (encomium) and blame, but in general usage all ceremonial or occasional oratory 10, 102

epilogos (ἐπίλογος): 'epilogue'; the closing (often emotional) part of a speech, following the main argumentation (cf *koinē poiotēs, telika kephalaia*) 50, 55, 62, 68, 96, 102, 105

eschēmatismenos logos (ἐσχηματισμένος λόγος): 'figured speech', i.e. one in which the speaker's real purpose differs from his ostensible one 36

ēthopoiia (ἠθοποιΐα): 'representation of character', esp. the composition of 'the words that X might speak' (οὓς ἂν εἴποι λόγους) in a given situation; a *progymnasma* (q.v.), but also a frequent element in declamation 11, 54, 82, 99

ēthos (ἦθος): 'character' including not only the moral personality of an individual, but e.g. age, sex, profession, status or wealth 72, 122, ch. 5 passim

euthydikia (εὐθυδικία): 'primary case', i.e. the trial of the actual charge, as distinct from the proceedings of a *paragraphē* (q.v.), by which an attempt is made to prevent the original issue from being heard 62

gnōmē nomothetou (γνώμη νομοθέτου): 'lawgiver's intention' 52, 69

horos (ὅρος): 'definition'; as a *stasis*, an issue which turns on the question whether an action falls within the definition (legal or commonly accepted) of the offence alleged 51, 53

horos antonomazōn (ὅρος ἀντονομάζων): 'definition with change of name'; a type of issue exemplified by the man who has stolen private property from a temple and claims to be punished as a simple thief, not as one who has committed sacrilege 42, 52, 53

Technical terms

horos kata syllēpsin (ὅρος κατὰ σύλληψιν): 'definition by inclusion', i.e. when it is to be shown that the act in dispute is a species of a genus of acts falling under the definition in question 53

horos paragraphikos (ὅρος παραγραφικός): 'definition as demurrer', i.e. a *paragraphē* (q.v.) sustained by a definition 59, 101

hypokrisis (ὑπόκρισις): 'delivery' 82

hypothesis (ὑπόθεσις)
  (i) subject of declamation 85
  (ii) summary or plot of speech or play 119

kakoplastos (κακόπλαστος): 'wrongly devised', 'ill-conceived', a term used of anachronistic or implausible declamation themes (cf *asystatos*) 114

katastasis (κατάστασις): 'situation', i.e. a narrative establishing the circumstances of the case, normally inserted immediately after the prologue 54, 61, 64, 66, 67, 88 (esp. n. 6), 91, 98, 125

kephalaion (κεφάλαιον): 'head', 'chapter' (cf *telika kephalaia*) 72

koinē poiotēs (κοινὴ ποιότης): 'common quality', a term covering the general emotional evaluation and *telika kephalaia* (q.v.) appropriate to the *epilogos* (q.v.) 50

komma (κόμμα): a 'comma', i.e. a single phrase, shorter than a *kōlon*; so adv. *kommatikōs* (κομματικῶς) means 'in short phrases', 'in a staccato manner' 94

lalia (λαλιά): 'talk' (cf *dialexis*) 77

meletē (μελέτη): 'practice', 'exercise', the usual term in Greek for 'declamation' 10 and passim

metalēpsis (μετάληψις)
  (i) as a *stasis* (Lat. *translatio*), the position that the case ought not to be tried by the present procedure (cf *paragraphē*) 7, 45, 60, 61
  (ii) as a detail of a speech, 'counter-plea', the answer to an *antilēpsis* (q.v.); see also *enstasis*, *antiparastasis* 45, 48, 60, 69

metastasis (μετάστασις): 'transference', a defendant's attempt to shift blame to someone else or to external circumstances over which he himself had not control; not always clearly distinguished from *antenklēma* (q.v.) 7, 17, 58, 66

metathesis aitias (μετάθεσις αἰτίας): 'transposition of cause'; the defendant alleges a reason which justifies the action for which he is being tried (cf *chrōma*) 48

mimēsis (μίμησις): 'imitation' of life or of classical literary models 109

nomikai staseis (νομικαὶ στάσεις): 'legal issues', as distinct from those of reasoning (*logikai staseis*, q.v.), subdivided into *rhēton kai dianoia*, *antinomia amphibolia*, *syllogismos* (qq.v.) 56

parabolē (παραβολή): 'example'; distinguished from *paradeigma* (q.v.) as being taken from general facts of the natural world, not from past history 101

paradeigma (παράδειγμα): 'example', strictly one taken from history or mythology (cf *parabolē*) 101

paragraphē, *paragraphikon* (παραγραφή, παραγραφικόν): vb παραγράφεσθαι, 'to enter a demurrer'): 'demurrer', i.e. objection to the bringing of the case before the present court (see also *metalēpsis*, *euthydikia*) 38, 45, 101, 121

pēlikotēs (πηλικότης): 'size', 'importance', 'gravity': the point that an action (usually the offence) is in itself a very serious or momentous matter (cf *pros ti*) 52, 54, 61

periechon kai periechomenon (περιέχον καὶ περιεχόμενον): 'including and included', an argument used in cases of *amphibolia* (q.v.), showing, e.g., that if a person becomes a public slave, that person's property also belongs to the public 69

pithanē apologia (πιθανὴ ἀπολογία): 'persuasive (or 'plausible') defence': esp. the use by a defendant of a fact relied upon by the prosecution, showing that it really supports the defence case (see also *biaios horos*) 49, 128

plasma (πλάσμα): 'fiction', the usual term for the invented scenario of a declamation which has no specific historical setting; also, a declamation of this kind 5, 103, 106

poiotēs (ποιότης: Lat. *qualitas*)
    (i) a general name for any *stasis* in which the point at issue is not the fact or definition but the 'quality' of the action under dispute 55
    (ii) see *koinē poiotēs*
    (iii) 'quality' in general, e.g. the character of a party to the case 53

pragmatikē (πραγματικὴ στάσις): any *logikē stasis* (q.v.) which 'concerns the future', and thus the 'issue' to which deliberative speeches can be assigned (cf *dikaiologia*) 7, 56, 63, 94, 97

probolē (προβολή): the actual 'statement' or 'presentation' of the charge, Lat. *intentio criminis*; often immediately following the *katastasis* (q.v.) 52, 54

progymnasma (προγύμνασμα): 'elementary exercise'; Hermogenes' list gives fable (*mythos*), narration (*diēgēma*), anecdote (*chreia*), maxim (*gnōmē*), refutation (*anaskeuē*), confirmation (*kataskeuē*), commonplace (*koinos topos*), encomium (*enkōmion*), comparison (*synkrisis*), *ēthopoiia* (q.v.), *ekphrasis* (q.v.), thesis (q.v.), and 'introduction of law' (*nomou eisphora*) 11, 71, 102, 122

prokataskeuazomenos (προκατασκευαζόμενος): 'preliminary'; used of a *stochasmos* or *horos* (qq.v.) which has to be dealt with before the main issue can be argued (contrast *empiptōn*, *synkataskeuazomenos*, qq.v.) 50

prolalia (προλαλιά): 'introductory talk' (cf *lalia*) 77

prooimion (προοίμιον): 'introduction', 'prologue', i.e. the first part of a speech, normally preceding the narrative (when the plural *prooimia* is used, the meaning is that the speech has more than one 'introductory theme') 54, 125

prosangelia (προσαγγελία): 'denunciation', esp. 'self-denunciation' (vb ἑαυτὸν προσαγγέλλειν), i.e. declaring to the authorities that one wishes to be allowed the means of suicide (usually poison), because circumstances have made life unbearable; a common scenario of *plasmata* (q.v.), supposed to be based on the actual law of some Greek cities 35, 63, 91, 96

pros ti (πρός τι): lit. 'in relation to something'; the topic of the *relative* importance or gravity of an action or offence, contrasted with its absolute importance (*pēlikotēs*, q.v.) 52, 55

rhēton kai dianoia (ῥητὸν καὶ διάνοια): 'letter and intention' (i.e. 'spirit') of a law: a *nomikē stasis* (q.v.); also an argument on these lines deployed in any case, one party's insistence on the letter being answered by appealing to intention, and vice versa (cf *gnōmē nomothetou*) 61, 65

sententia: Lat. term for a pithy remark of general application, apt in the particular situation of the speech; Gk equivalent is *gnōmē*. Also an excercise consisting of a discussion of such a sentiment (cf *progymnasmata*) 2, 86

stasis (στάσις: Lat. *status* or *constitutio*): 'issue' involved in a case (lit. 'stance' or perhaps 'quarrel') 3, 6, 17, 40ff
stochasmos (στοχασμός: Lat. *coniectura*): 'conjecture'), i.e. 'issue of fact', where the case depends on determining whether the defendant did the deed 42, 44, 124
suasoria: Lat. term for a deliberative declamation, i.e. one in which the speaker gives advice in a defined historical situation (cf *pragmatikē stasis*) 4, 106
syllogismos (συλλογισμός)
   (i) 'inference' (from the wording of a law), a variety of *nomikē stasis* (q.v.) 70
   (ii) 'inference' or 'implication' more generally 52, 54, 62
synēgoros (συνήγορος): 'advocate', i.e. a speaker who supports or represents a litigant 14
syngnōmē (συγγνώμη): 'pardon'; the defendant's plea to be pardoned, though he admits his guilt, because of extenuating circumstances (often his state of mind) 7, 59
synkataskeuazomenos (συγκατασκευαζόμενος): 'linked'; applied to a question of fact (*stochasmos*) or of definition (*horos*), so related to another question that the case requires the establishment of both (contrast *empiptōn*, *prokataskeuazomenos*, qq.v.) 50

telika kephalaia (τελικὰ κεφάλαια: Lat. *finalia capitula*): 'final headings', i.e. 'headings of purpose', so called either because they are used at the end (*telos*, cf *koinē poiotēs*, *epilogos*) or (better) because they express the goal (*telos*) of actions: i.e. justice, legality, expediency, honour, pleasure, possibility and the like 50, 63
theōria (θεωρία): 'theory', 'theoretical explanation', esp. a teacher's preliminary exposition preceding declamation (also *protheōria*) 83
thesis (θέσις): a general proposition to be defended or attacked, distinct from 'hypothesis' (ὑπόθεσις), which is a specific theme about specified persons and places (see also *progymnasma*) 71, 102, 122

zētēma (ζήτημα): 'question', i.e. the problem set by the propounder of a subject for declamation 13, 43